Hudibras in the Burlesque Tradition

Hudibras

IN THE

Burlesque

Tradition

By EDWARD AMES RICHARDS

1972

OCTAGON BOOKS

New York

Reprinted 1972

by special arrangement with Columbia University Press

OCTAGON BOOKS

A DIVISION OF FARRAR, STRAUS & GIROUX, INC.

19 Union Square West

New York, N. Y. 10003

LIBRARY OF CONGRESS CATALOG CARD NUMBER: 77-154665

ISBN 0-374-96798-9

Printed in U.S.A. by

NOBLE OFFSET PRINTERS, INC.

NEW YORK 3, N. Y.

CONTENTS

ACKNOWLEDGMENT

I AM deeply grateful to my wife for her abundant possession of those qualities demanded of, but rarely found in, those women who marry students; to the members of the Department of English in Columbia University, who are distinguished for patience as for knowledge, particularly to Professor Frank A. Patterson, to whom I am indebted for guidance in matters far beyond the narrow limits of this book, and to Professor William G. Haller and Dr. Henry Wells for their friendly and critical advice; to the members of the staff at the Columbia Library, the New York Public Library, the Widener Library, the Bodleian, and the British Museum, for their courteous assistance; and, finally, to Miss Katharine M. Gault for her aid in preparing the manuscript and in correcting the proofs.

EDWARD A. RICHARDS

COLUMBIA UNIVERSITY
IN THE CITY OF NEW YORK
April 2, 1937

INTRODUCTION

EVERYONE who has read Samuel Butler's *Hudibras* has praised the book and the author, and such praise is comely; for the poem is one of the great burlesques in English literature. The book is available for anyone to read, but the author of it has come down to us wrapped in an almost medieval obscurity. He wrote nothing about himself, his contemporaries say little about him, and he has therefore lived in the shadow of his own art. There is a refreshing quality in this very fact, but it has left to us the difficulty of visualizing the sort of man and the sort of mind that lie behind *Hudibras*. Mr. Veldkamp and Mr. de Beer have, indeed, furnished good biographical accounts of Butler, in addition to Johnson's critical *Life*. Neither of these works, however, nor the many others which treat *Hudibras* primarily, are designed to describe and to interpret the attitude of Butler toward the constant intellectual problems of government, religion, philosophy and art. This book begins with attempting such an interpretation, chiefly through the study of Butler's writing aside from *Hudibras*, namely the *Characters* and the *Satires and Miscellaneous Poetry and Prose*. Impersonal as these pieces are, they are of considerable importance in getting at least a clear outline of what kind of man the author of *Hudibras* was.

The obscurity of Butler as a person is almost matched by that surrounding the relation of *Hudibras* to later burlesques. It is well known that the hudibrastic fashion was continued after Butler's death, that Ward, Prior, Swift and Trumbull used Butler's meter, and that burlesque writing enjoyed general popularity for a long time. But the bearing of Butler's poem on these productions, the place of *Hudibras* in literary history, have not been stated in a way at once clear and connected. Such a statement this book attempts to supply.

The political poems which take their manner and some of their matter from *Hudibras* are written, on the whole, from the Tory or Conservative point of view; one seldom hears an insurgent note in them. This is their distinctive mark. How this point of view was expressed hudibrastically in relation to political and social questions between 1680 and 1830 is the subject of the second part of this book.

The form of those questions naturally changed with time, and so did the feeling if not the form of hudibrastic verse. I have tried to show, chiefly in the last part of the present study, how other temperaments and other literary fashions affected the verse form of Butler. In doing so I have had to venture a few suggestions on what produces the burlesque mood in literature and what the effect of that mood may be, with only casual recourse to the definition of burlesque by types such as the parody, the travesty, and the mock-heroic. Driven by this effort into a confusing field of esthetic relativities, I have taken refuge in a working division of the subject that is no doubt over-simplified, but that seems to me useful.

The chief conclusions on this subject are that burlesque is an intentional distortion of an action or an idea; that the basis of it may be either dramatic or intellectual, but is generally dramatic; that it is chiefly critical in purpose, more intellectual than moral; and that it may be produced either by realistic or by imaginative methods. These statements are, obviously, not intended to be a sure formula for all burlesque, based as they are on the style of the works discussed in this book. I believe, nevertheless, that consideration of them will help to place *Hudibras* in clearer literary perspective, and will have some general validity outside the tradition of that poem.

Part One

SAMUEL BUTLER

I

TEMPERAMENT AND OPINIONS

WHEN, as Mr. Trevelyan says, "the comic spirit had landed" in England with Charles II, a great opportunity lay within reach of anyone with comic talents as great as those of Samuel Butler. Not only the demand for wit at court but the intellectual temper of the age was in his favor. He was a man of wide polite learning, active intelligence, and skeptical temper, and not long after the Restoration he published an almost incredibly witty poem burlesquing the politically discredited Presbyterians and Independents—a book that delighted the King. Nevertheless, this brilliant son of a yeoman farmer never reached during his life a personal eminence commensurate with the undoubted fame of his book. We do not find him in the center of any group, whether of the philosophers, or the scientists, or the literary men. He is not owned by the court, or by society, or by the party politicians. While he satirized the Dissenters, he seems, from whatever cause, to have endured an incurable separateness in his own person and in his own mind.

No doubt his interest in party lines and party fights was not avid enough to make his advancement of prime importance. In spite of his rough treatment of Presbyterian and Independent, he was by no means a bigoted Anglican or a blind royalist; his intellectual designs were far wider than those of a partisan pamphleteer. Butler, practically without the capacity for active identification with current concerns, was isolated in his own cold and scornful mind. There was an unchanging, frozen quality in the mind and temper of this artist-philosopher, a quality beyond re-

straint, that indeed would have made restraint meaningless—an unshakable, inactive and scornful rationalism that
discounted all claims of party, and that was incapable of
lending itself with genuine enthusiasm to any cause, or
movement, or hope, or prophecy. From this remoteness he
issued short, smoothly clipped essays against the objects
of his distaste and succeeded in dovetailing many of these
to make the poem, or, if you prefer, the series of poems,
called *Hudibras*. He could not escape his own temperament
any more than any other man; and men of scornful and remote tempers do not win personal acclaim and popularity,
nor are they likely to be very adaptable to political require-
ments and to shifts in literary taste. Butler pursued a somewhat covert career, and if his book was more popular than
he himself, one of the chief causes resided in his own
temperament.

Interesting and significant is the variety of groups to
win this author's sour distrust. His dislike of Presbyterians
and Dissenters is well known and merits analysis later in
this chapter. On the other hand, Catholicism like the sects
seems to him the religion fitted for the mass, the "rabble";
with the difference that this organization is cannily ad-
ministered from above with no attempt to encourage political ambition in its communicants. There is not much to
choose, however, among all the parties of religion; the
church of compromises and governmental convenience,
the Anglican Church, is hardly to be preferred over the
rest. The interpretation and administration of the law of
God leaves much to be desired.

For though God made Religion, as Princes and Governments do
Laws, yet they who have the management, and interpreting of
both, will make what they please of either. Nor is it probable that
the Laws of God should fare better than those of Magistrates, who
are present to oversee their execution, while the Ministers of the

other, are left wholly to themselves in this world and only ac-
comptable in the next.[1]

Therefore, the bishops since the Restoration have by their
zeal in consolidating their required power antagonized
afresh the Dissenting elements in the population, and are in
a fair way to destroy the effects of the English Reformation. "These officers and commanders of the Church
Militant, are like Souldiers of Fortune that are free to serve
on any Side that gives the best Pay." It will appear later
that Butler owned a sincere religion, part agnostic, part
deistic, and therefore one need not be surprised at his
cynical regard for the various religious organizations. The
point is important here because it seems to emphasize his
lack of any sort of conventional allegiance and means of
social identification. "It is both the wisest," Butler says,
"and the Safest way in the world to keep at a Convenient
Distance with all men."

The man who cannot or who does not identify himself
with overt social groups is quite likely to take refuge in
some private intellectual concern, especially if he possesses
an intellectual genius. Butler, however, found scant comfort in the contemporary intellectual concerns. Divinity
was too contentious, and like metaphysics too abstruse, to
satisfy his sense of reality; on the other hand, current
scientists were too quixotic and gullible in some of their
activities—irrational, in short. From every side Butler
was driven back to his own sardonic pessimism, and to a
circuit of ideas confused by contrariety and paradox.

Of certain positive ideas and beliefs, however, he was
very tenacious; they are stated repeatedly, though most
frequently in that oblique and allusive phraseology that is
so distinctive a feature of *Hudibras*. It should be worth our
while to review these beliefs at some length, since they are

[1] Unless otherwise noted, all quotations in Part One are from *Characters and Passages from Note-Books*.

interesting in themselves, and since they are specifically important to any general revaluation of the author's chief poem. The exposition may most conveniently begin with an account of Butler's philosophical statements concerning "nature," "reality," and the general problem of whether we know anything, and if we do, how we come to know it. These problems are not handled by Butler in the manner of a professional philosopher. They must be considered here chiefly because they are fundamental to his views on divinity, on the state, and on the nature of man.

Our satirist believes that truth exists and that it can be arrived at by human intelligence, difficult though the attainment of it may be. The exposition of his views would undoubtedly have been clearer had he been able to consider all experience, like society, as an organic thing. His theory of what truth is runs repeatedly into the assumption that truth is of two kinds, rational and revealed, secular and divine, in that troublesome dichotomy which must always apparently in one form or another bedevil the human spirit. Here is God, a quasi-legal divinity; here again is "Nature," a protean force, equally hard to define in positive terms. In practical thinking, the former term represents the center of those forces or "laws" which operate in all phenomena, particularly in the phenomena of human living, but which have no unique physical home and center of existence. Of this transcendent truth we can know little or nothing. Immanent truth is "Nature." It is the eternal force reduced to the temporal, imbedded in "first matter"; and first matter is the miraculous and immanent vestige of transcendent truth: "All things were hidden in the first Matter," says Butler, "as a Bird is in an Egge; But now it is hidden in all things, as an Egge is in a Bird," here making good use of the ancient hen-and-egg controversy, and suggesting why he scorned those philosophers who pretended to have surprised first matter "all alone, before a rag of

Form was on." Now this derivative, physically embodied, and in a sense physically concealed, form of truth can be perceived and apprehended in part by man.

In this temporal and physical existence, "the specificall Principles of things" proceeding from first matter, exert their power. There are no interstices in the fabric of Nature through which the fire of transcendency can be glimpsed. Still, there is no lack of happenings that seem to be beyond nature, and the mongers of supernatural wonder, for their own several purposes, dwell too much on the ocean of man's ignorance that surrounds the island of his knowledge.

The Ignorance of Naturall Causes make's many things passe for Miracles that are not so, and when they are once reputed Miraculous, The many who are always inclined to favour strang[e] things do their endevour to make as much of them as they can.

Knowledge cannot be had by means of logic—an art that can teach men "only little Tricks and evasions"— but can be attained solely by "a right observation of Nature." And "the end of all Knowledge, is to understand what is Fit to be don; For to know what has been, and what is, and what may be, dos but tend to that." This definition does not take into much account the inferential or rational part of knowledge, and suggests a distinction in Butler's mind between knowledge and truth.

"Truth," we learn, "is too strict and severe to make Parties, and Factions, and want[s] that free latitude to flourish in, which error always usurps: For there is too little of it known to make any great appearance in the world." This truth, indeed, has no absolute existence, nor does it have to do with the correct observation of any single phenomenon. It consists rather in the right relationship among ideas. "Truth is scarce so much as a Notion, for it is but the Putting of those Notions of things (in the understanding of Man) into the same order that their Originals are in Nature." Obviously, the attainment and the recognition of truth is a different operation from that of knowledge, and requires the act of reason for its fulfillment. The human mind includes all those faculties by which the knowledge is obtained and reasoned upon; though by one faculty, definitely proceeding

from the Divine wisdom, put's the Notions, and Images of things (with their operations, effects, and Circumstances) that are confus'd in the understanding, into the same order and condition, in which they are really dispos'd by Nature, or event: The Right Performance of this is cald Truth, to which Reason naturally tend's in a direct line, although she sometime miscarry, and faile by the Subtlety of the Object, or her own Imperfection; and that we call error or Falshood.

Between the entirely true and the entirely false is the domain of wit which "by a certaine slight of the Minde, deliver's things otherwise then they are in Nature, by rendering them greater or lesse then they really are." And the domain of wit is a good deal the same as that of opinion; neither has to do with the separation of truth from falsehood, while each is a superficial means of persuading oneself and one's companions that a certain matter is true or false, without reference to actual knowledge. The defect of wit and of opinion, in spoken and written thought, is the defect of substituting the word for the thing, the shadow for the substance.

For those who propose wit, and Fancy for their end, and take in sense and Reason only as circumstantiall and on the by, judge as extravagantly as those who believe themselves Rich, because they can cast up ever so great Sums of Money, but have not one Penny.

The vagaries of the reason itself, then, divine though its source may be, as well as the imperfections of sense and the "Subtlety of the Object," blur the infrequent image of truth. But this is not all; imagination and opinion actually assail the reason and bring it to confusion. The former cheate's the Senses, and rayses the Passions to that prodigious height, that . . . it transport's a man beyond himself, and do's things so far beside the ordinary Course of Nature, and the understanding of the wisest, that as if they had lost their wits too by contagion, it often passe's for possessions of the Devill.

Imagination prevents men from seeing things as they are, but it is not the fertile field for imposture that opinion is, for opinion prevents men from asserting what they plainly see to be true. Opinion imposes a "Restraint so ungratefull to Reason . . . that commonly her best performances, are but canting, and imposture."

This brief review shows Butler to be a man of cautious and skeptical intellect, a pragmatist and a rationalist, unlikely to forget the imperfections of sense, the difficulty of right reason, the "Subtlety of the Object," the scarcely penetrable secrets of the physical universe. It shows him, too, on his guard against enthusiasms of the imagination, and against the fearful pressures which reason must resist if she would do her duty in a society where nearly every public and overt act is performed by policy against a background of apprehension. "Jealousies and fears" were by no means the sole property of the rebellious parties in the forties. They came more and more to condition the actions of men after the uneasy Restoration. And I am inclined to believe that Butler's abhorrence of the compromises of political life helped to bar him from the prominence which a man of his abilities might have been expected to reach in an age that set so great store on a man's "parts."

His rationalistic approach to truth is naturally paralleled in his attitude toward religion, where reason is again the dominant force. He will have nothing to do with religious truth come at by any kind of revelation but that achieved through the cautious processes of the mind.

Faith can determine nothing of Reason, but Reason can of Faith. . . . Faith cannot define Reason, but Reason can Faith. . . . No man can believe anything but because he do's not know it . . . the lesse any man knowes the more he hath to believe.

In religion perhaps more than in any other interest of humanity, opinion is the greatest check upon progress. "For all men agree in the end of Religion that God is to be worshiped," but differences in doctrine and in method have divided religious people into warring groups. Religion seems to Butler to be quite simply the worship of God. As to any other positive belief on the matter he leaves us in the dark. He makes no guesses concerning the nature of God, nor the substance of the law of God. He has little to say about the New Testament, and on the whole question of Biblical authority his remarks are confused and contradictory. Quite plainly, the laws of God are contained in Holy Writ, with many evidences of the way in which they work. But who shall say precisely what these laws are, and what man on earth shall judge other men in accordance with the presumed will of God? The problem certainly is no novel one, and Butler's solution is no clearer than most. Conscience will reprove a man for his misdoings on earth, and conscience is cognizant through the reason of that moral philosophy on which the Christian religion "may seem to have" its base. But no one on earth can say whether a man be damned or saved here or hereafter; no church can do so, for the officers of all churches are in some sense special pleaders:

Certainly Almighty God will not be so unmerciful (since his Mercy is above all his workes) to Mankinde, to expose the eternall Being of Soules, to the Passion, Interest, and Ignorance, of those that make themselves his Messengers, and do their owne work in his Name.

This passage should, I believe, be held to apply to churches generally, since nowhere, as far as I can find, does Butler indicate a belief that the Anglican or any other sect has been singled out by God as a unique conduit for His truth.

Again, the text of the Bible is so old as to allow of many different constructions, and this difficulty, together with the separatist tendency in mankind, leads to inescapable wars of opinion. Religious truth, like all other truth, is really simple and plain; but the churches built on it, or rather near it, are ornate and stormy in design. In a way it would have been better had the Christian church never grown in strength and in its doctrinal rigidities. In its early days it was forced to be truly catholic and to take many heresies into the body of the church which in its later authoritarian days it neither wished nor needed to do. Heresy, which is nothing but "the Disease of Different Constitutions and Capacitys," could hardly fail to continue in the race and to multiply churches. The churches finding most of their strength in faith, and most men being committed by their "Capacitys" to ignorance and the sway of opinion, made such a union as drew great ignorant multitudes into the churches in the name of faith. And these churches of the ignorant faithful, or the faithful ignorant (either phrase would, in Butler's view, be redundant) are governed in the name of God by men as shrewd, as powerful, as self-seeking, as fleshly, as avaricious and corrupt as any other class of men alive. No church escapes censure. "The Romish Religion is best fitted to the Capacitys of the Ignorant Rabble" through its fables; the Church of England is vindictive, venal, and greedy; the Dissenters are the ignorant and corrupt led by the ignorant and corrupt. Among men generally "Fools have always the strongest fayths," and the layman has as little chance of gaining a crumb of secular truth as the clergy has of knowing and interpreting the will of God. Nevertheless, man's reliance can be only on reason, which by attempting to view experience in its true order and its exact relationships, approaches the truth. To this inclusive operation the apprehension of religious and moral truth is incidental. The images of religion, the cathedrals and conventicles, have nothing to do with this central effort. They are built to God in the name of that ignorance which is the buttress of faith. Who could have ever supposed that faith is "the substance of things hoped for"!

Man, in Butler's view, is in truth essentially a hopeless animal. The naturalistic view of the race and the mood concomitant with that view overshadow the occasional piety of his remarks.

There is no Creature so much a Slave to his own condition as man, that owes his Being to Fancy and his wel-being to Fortune; That is made by the Sun to be burnt up with his Rays, or betray'd by him to the Cold: that is exposed Naked to all the Cruelty's of Heaven and Earth, beside those greater that men inflict upon one another. That is sentenced to the horrid execution of Death, with so much uncertainty of his after condition, that the Differences of Men about the next Life, become their greatest Troubles in this, where though their best Certaintys are but Hopes and beliefs, yet every man is so confident, that he is ready to beat out any man's Braines that do not agree with his owne. That hath all his pleasures imaginary, and his Paines Reall, His Calamitys and Afflictions that come of themselves, but his emoluments and Security not without great care and Industry. That is forced to drudge for that Food and Clothing which other creatures receive freely from the Bounty of Nature.

This creature inhabits with his reason a thin grayish strip of shore between the dark continent of his senses and the dark ocean of the universe, and does what he can to hold his own.

To do so, man botches other institutions besides the Church. Of these none is quite so necessary nor quite so evil as the state. Within the state, all government is tyranny, the chief distinction resting between a light tyranny and a burdensome one. Butler has seen political dominance swing from king, to parliament, to army, and back again to monarchy, and wearily concludes that

All Governments are in their Managements so equall, that no one has the advantage of another, unless in Speculation, and in that there is no convenience that any Particular Model can Pretend to, but is as liable to as great Inconveniences some other way.

Thus a tyranny is theoretically bad, but actually may be good if the tyrant is beneficient; also, commonwealths are notoriously poor rewarders of public service, "yet they are generally better serv'd then Princes," who reserve honor and gain chiefly to themselves and their descendants.

Behind all actions of state is the desire of the sovereign to hold the people together as a united nation, frequently inciting them to hate all foreigners, but always by converting

the Ignorance, Folly, and Madness of Mankinde (as much as may be) to their own good, which can never be don, by telling them Truth and Reason, or using any direct meanes; but by little Tricks and Divises (as they cure Mad men) that worke upon their Hopes and Feares to which their Ignorance naturally incline's them.

This process calls, of course, for a deep and exact knowledge of people, singly and in the mass, if the government is to play upon their feelings in the right way at the right time, and calls for the fundamental virtue of hypocrisy and hidden design inherent in all "applied psychology." Hence it comes to pass that there can be little truly glorious in the history of nations; at the center they are all crooked.

Publique Actions are like watches that have fine Cases of Gold, or Silver, with a windore of Christall to see the Pretences, but the Movement is of Baser Mettle, and the Original of all (the Spring) a Crooked piece of Steel: So in the Affaires of State, The solemn Professions of Religion, Justice, and Liberty are but Pretences, to conceale Ambition, Rapine, and usefull Cheate.

This public world, barren of probity, offers a peculiar opportunity for the vices of monarchy. For the king chooses his advisers not on account of their ability, but out of love of flattery, or of entertainment, or because he likes their persons. No man need hope for preferment because he is wise or good; it is better for his fortune to be ignorant and dishonest; particularly in an age in which the men of noble birth perform their iniquities on the house-tops, an age which "will serve to make a very pretty Farce for the Next, if it have any Witt at all to make Use of it." Butler rarely writes directly about contemporary events, but he says enough about them to make it almost obliga-tory on the reader to give contemporary weight to general observations. His estimate of the reign of Charles II is given in the light of his general opinion of humanity, and no doubt tended to reinforce and embitter a cynicism al-ready thoroughly intrenched. He compliments Charles for having fewer legitimate sons than illegitimate as an in-stance of the trouble the King takes to insure a legal succession—the few are easier to keep track of; he sneers at Clarendon for favoring rebels and accepting their bribes in exchange for pardon and power; he flouts the open-minded clergy who "would have all Men have Religion enough to serve their own Interests, and no more"; he jeers at the Test Act as a most fruitful soil for the growth of that hypocrisy on which political hopes thrive.

As soon as a Man has taken an Oath against his Conscience and done his Endeavour to damn himself, He is capable of any Trust or Employment in the Government; So excellent a Quality is Perjury to render the most perfedious of Men most fit and proper for publick Charges of the greatest Consequence, . . . this is the Modern Way of Test as they call it—to take measure of Men's abilities and Faith by their Alacrity in Swearing—and is indeed the most Compendious way to exclude all those that have any Conscience, and to take in Such as have None at all.

There is nothing hopeful in the affairs of the kingdom. A careless king heads a licentious court, a venal church, and a people enjoying the shadow of liberty. For

Princes ought to give their Subjects as much of the Shadow of Liberty as they can for their lives, but as little of the Reality of it, if they regard the Safety of themselves or their People.

Furthermore, none of the subjects ought to suppose that by taking thought to set up a "new model" of government they can improve on the maleficent system in force. For effective governments are the product not of logic and of intellect, but of multifarious growth and slow change. "Governments are made like Natural Productions by Degrees according as their Materials are brought in by time." Hence, Butler disliked the civil wars, not because he admired the restored régime of the Stuarts, but because the wars were the product of jealous interests and of doctrinaire logic using the instruments of war. The product in his opinion was bound to be too mechanical and artificial to accord with what he considered to be the possible conditions of social and political growth. One can perhaps fairly sum up his attitude toward the state by comparing it with that of Hobbes. Butler tries to be and generally succeeds in being as cool, as secular, and as objective as his contemporary. But he is far more conservative in feeling; and whereas Hobbes considers any *de facto* government a government *de jure*, Butler insists that the lack of a just title in the Commonwealth doomed that government as a lasting English device. He is furthermore far more moralistic in his thinking, as he is less severe and systematic, and tends to see the rise and fall of princes depending on principles of moral right. And although he likes to use impersonal mechanical terms in speaking of public matters, he does so against a background of temperamental melancholy, a kind of suppressed mysticism, and what might be called a cultural despair, that betray a troubled agnosticism and a grudge against the unfortunate depravity of human kind.

All the Business of this World [he says] is but Diversion, and all the Happiness in it, that Mankind is capable of—anything that will keep it from reflecting upon the Misery, Vanity, and Nonsence of it: And whoever can by any Trick keep himself from Thinking of it, is as wise and Happy as the best Man in it.

The same kind of grudging and pessimistic criticism appears when Butler alludes to his literary contemporaries and to their manner of writing. One might say that his principal literary enthusiasms were negative. No writer claims his full approval. His objections to modern writers are directed against foreign, unoriginal subject matter, and against a style that seems to him pedantic, pretentious, deceptive, and untrue. Without meaning to be tart, we can fairly say that the only style that is to his mind really adequate is his own. He devotes what I believe to be his only directly autobiographical remark to this very subject:

My writings are not set of with the Ostentation of Prologue, Epilogue nor Preface, nor Sophisticated with Songs and Dances, nor Musique nor fine women between the Cantos; Nor have any thing to commend them but the Plaine Downrightness of the Sense.

Evidently Butler felt about style as he felt about truth, that the constituent parts of it should never be hard to come by. First-rate wit lies "so directly before [the writer] that he could not possibly avoid it." Unforced and unpretentious expression, free of stylistic curiosities and brief and clear, is ideal. *Hudibras* shows, despite its length, that the author succeeded more often than he failed in reaching his own ideal. For figurative decoration appears but seldom for its own sake, the clauses, even when long, sound terse, and comparisons however startling they may appear at first glance, seem obvious enough once Butler has woven them into the rhythms of his poem.

In the scholarly strife over ancient or modern culture our poet is distinctly on the side of the moderns and of the modern English. He has little or nothing to say about classic style, though his notebook is full of notes on Latin authors; these notes are largely statements of fact or fable which seem to be possible poetical material. He cries out against those who adulterate the English tongue, while seeking to enrich it, by using French terms; in criticism, again, the English poet should be judged, not by "Pedants, and Philosophers,"[2] but by his peers—in other words, by other English poets. Butler's own criticism of his peers is fragmentary, but none the less interesting and significant. He is fond of both Jonson and Shakespeare, though he remarks that the former, having "more Patience and Flegme," achieved a greater degree of perfection. The comment is not, of course, unique. On the other hand, his note on Donne is an extraordinary piece of criticism, both descriptive and impressionistic:

Dr. Don's writings are like Voluntary or Prelude in which a man is not ty'd to any particular Design of Air; but may change his key or moode at pleasure: So his compositions seem to have been written without any particular Scope.

It is notable that he has no reproof for Donne's rhetorical devices, reserving his disapproval for Waller, who expresses

Sense by Contradiction, and Riddle. Of this Mr. Waller, who was the first most copious Author, and has so infected our modern writers of Heroiques with it, that they can hardly write any other way, and if at any time they indeavour to do it, like Horses that are put out of their Pace, they presently fall naturally into it again. Trotto d'Asino dura poco.

Butler accused Denham of having "bought *Cooper's Hill*," and of having "borrow'd Sophy,"[3] and he nowhere says a word in favor of the dominant talent and popularity of Dryden. This author in fact is perhaps alluded to in the many passages in Butler which remark contemptuously on the current dramatic borrowings from France and Spain. This is the point at least of the single passage in which Dryden is called by name:

Dryden weighs Poets in the virtuoso's Scales that will turne

[2] *Satires*, p. 62.
[3] *Satires*, p. 120.

with the hundredth part of a Graine as Curiously as Juvenal's Lady Poedantesse

> Committit vates, et comparat inde Maronem
> Atque alia parte in trutina suspendit Homerum.

He complayned of B. Johnson for stealing 40 Sceanes out of Plautus. Set a Thief to finde out a Thiefe.

When Butler does not thus sound a note of suspicion about the work of his contemporaries, he attacks them outright. He charges Milton with the defect of paying no attention to thè merits of the case in his debate with Salmasius, but of acting like a mere polemic in attacking only the language of his rival. He laughs at Hobbes for setting too great store by his own intellect and for believing that the earlier publication of *De cive* would have prevented the outbreak of civil war. It is hard to say with whom Butler could have felt sympathy. His criticism of these men, either for not being honest literary artists, or for not being sensible and forthright political realists, suggests again a narrow social and artistic field for Butler himself to enlarge himself in. As he is variously unwilling to cry out Credo for anything in religion or politics, so he appears cool to all existing literary manners.

A sense of that not very happy sort of independence called isolation is suggested by the foregoing paragraphs; and if this inference is a right one, it follows that *Hudibras* is not primarily nor principally a burlesque of Dissent. Certainly Dissent is burlesqued in the poem, and just as certainly the first readers of the work considered it to be a partisan attack on the record and the peculiarities of the submerged Presbyterians and sectaries. In the light of all of Butler's writing that has been preserved, however, *Hudibras* seems to be only incidentally a partisan attack. It becomes clear that Butler was writing not from the point of view of the Anglican Church, nor from the point of view of the court, but from the point of view of his own

mind—a mind unsympathetic, agnostic, socially disillu-
sioned—and that from a world that he saw full of absurd,
venal and dangerous parties, he chose the most absurd
and potentially the most dangerous. There is no more
need to deny the convenience of his subject matter than to
question his sincerity. Presbyterians and Independents
were no longer parties in any political sense; they were, indeed, ghosts which would be revitalized for political purposes during the next half century, but which were then
recently dead and the quieter therefor. It would have been,
correspondingly, most inconvenient for Butler to have
satirized the Anglicans, but it would also have been consistent for him to have done so, both on account of his own
views on religion, and of the sectarian nature of that church
after the Act of Uniformity. This omission, nevertheless,
by no means obscures his own position, nor does it invali-
date the satire of *Hudibras*. Butler sees mankind generally
as rabble led by literal-minded, vain and ignorant men in
power. In *Hudibras* he particularizes on this general theme.

I should distinguish six separate charges which the
satirist brings against Dissent: namely, hypocrisy, greed,
lust, intellectual narrowness, low social status, and a
foolish mysticism. There is no necessity to linger here over
the first three qualities since they are universal enough to
constitute the stock in trade of all satirists. The last three
are special and specific and they own a peculiar interest
since they in turn become, singly or in combination, stock
charges against Dissent after Butler's day. For instance,
the essential criticisms of Butler, of Matthew Arnold, and
of H. L. Mencken can be placed on one another and come
very near identity in spite of differences of time and of
culture. It is not, of course, to be expected that Butler's
picture should have been a fair one; the times were against
such a possibility; and, in any event, he was writing not a
critical history, but an artistic fable. On the other hand, it

may be well to remember the omissions which the author had to make in order to bring into his picture that element of distortion without which burlesque cannot exist. In regard to the moral issues of greed and lust for money and power, it can properly be said that the fight for the control of the church was of necessity largely economic on both sides. The power to have and to use church funds, church lands, and churchly political force was eagerly sought by Anglican and Puritan; and sincere as was the debate on ecclesiastical issues, the economic issue was a strong factor in the strife. In regard to doctrine, again, as distinguished from church government, the centers of Presbyterianism and of Independency were at no time far from the left wing of the Anglicans. The parties are difficult to distinguish; they melt into one another. This cloudiness of outline is also readily discernible in trying to determine those political and social cleavages which furnish the cutting edge to so much of Butler's satire. We may, I believe, attribute to our author a large share in fixing and popularizing the notion that there is a natural and inescapable connection among the ideas of Dissent, democracy, and ignorance. The omissions here are historically obvious enough; for it is clear that the leaders of Presbyterianism and Dissent were not democrats, nor were they part of an ignorant rabble. A large section of the Presbyterians were always Royalist in sympathy; indeed, they wanted a nationalist church of their own model, but were not politically able to make it stick. Even after the Restoration the majority in the House of Lords was by no means Anglican in its sympathies, and of course Cromwell himself had as few illusions as Butler concerning the political capacity of the man in the street. These matters suggest that the characterizations in *Hudibras* are something less than exact, particularly with respect to political actualities.

It is true, nevertheless, that no social satire can be successfully completed unless it has a basis that is socially and humanly real, and such realities are not lacking in the basis of *Hudibras*. The entire controversy over what settlement of government, both ecclesiastical and secular, should be made, is extraordinarily mechanical and legalistic. We may even go further and say that the dominant philosophy of the day inclined toward mechanism and legalism. Man as a mechanism in the thinking of Descartes, and the state as a mechanism in the theories of Hobbes, might be looked upon as isolated phenomena, were it not for the common contemporary assumption that both society and the state are structures or machines that are made to operate by the proper distribution and manipulation of the parts. The gradual deepening of party lines, and the strengthening of the boundaries of parties and of interests rather strengthened than weakened this attitude, leaving the political thinking of England for the next century in a dry and inorganic state. Now Butler, staunch intellectualist as he was, scorned the idea that essential changes could be made in church or state through the means of logical argument. Societies, he says in effect, are not made and unmade by theory. They are organic, with the illnesses and the possibilities of growth and of health which organisms possess. His analogy seems to us, even looking back at the Restoration from the vantage point of the machine age, to be more valid than the analogy of mechanism. At any rate, since he held this point of view, he was clearly bound to feel no enthusiasm for the Covenant nor for any instrument of government. They seemed to him to be, if not beside the point, at least outside the course of natural social development. At the same time, however, he could feel no special enthusiasm for the legalistic justification for the Restoration of the Stuart line. Butler's theory of political development is by no means clear, but he seems to have had a feeling about the development of English society which could not be satisfied by any party enthusiasm. If a phrase is needed, he might be called a political latitudinarian.

When Butler looks at the religious controversy, he sees, in the first place, arguments pro and con which rest either on the authority of the Bible, or on the authority of other books written thereafter, and he cannot but feel scornful of the entire matter. For what are books, on the whole, but opinion? And how slight the difference between an opinion and a belief! He does not at all believe that the strife over religion is a battle for the will of God, on either side. It is a battle over the differing opinions of men, and therefore futile. Nor must we neglect to add to these things the fact that the author of *Hudibras* was probably as sincere a pacifist as could have been found in his day outside the Quaker sect. At least he was certain that the trial by battle had nothing to do with the merits of causes brought to that stage for decision. The famous phrase "apostolic blows and knocks," while losing none of its savor and point, receives an extended meaning when read with the author's other remarks about wars. A war for God is an impossibility; a war for a righteous state cannot be waged, for no righteous state exists; no war can be a war for the cause of justice, since war and justice are incompatible. Wars are made for the sake of pride, of power, of money; war for the sake of any elevated notion involves an insuperable contradiction.

Granted that both parties of the Civil War pursued an illogical course, what was the special defect of the forces called Puritan? In the first place, they used violence in an attempt to enforce their opinions, thus upsetting the development of the nation; and, in the second place, there was an intellectual ignorance, as well as a political, involved in this attempt. Once started, they went from violence to violence, from logic to logic more and more inept and unreal, until violence came to an end in comparative rest, and logic was replaced by a condition which in spite of its ineptitudes was socially more real. The restored régime was in its turn hypocritical, violent, immoral, inept, but as its claims to validity were not so sweeping, neither were its overt political acts so violent.

This attempt to describe Butler's essential attitudes would be incomplete without reference to his disbelief in inspiration or new light. At first glance it seems strange that a man who cared so little for authoritarian views in religion should have held so bitter an antipathy toward the chance illuminations of the private man. Both antipathies are, however, quite in accord with his views of the nature of truth. The way of truth is not through another mind, nor can it be traveled easily by one's own mind. The truth that is found, and found but rarely, through observing certain relationships among objects, persons, and ideas, can certainly not be come at in a flash, especially by a person of no education. If anyone claims to receive truth in that way, he is a hypocrite and a charlatan, and no talk about the fatherhood of God and the spiritual stature of his chosen children will blur that fact.

II

A DISCUSSION OF HUDIBRAS

IN THE author of *Hudibras* we meet a man who claims our curiosity and respect rather than any warmth or excitement or allegiance. He owns less pity for the race than scorn, less humor than wit, less hope than stoicism. He has gained himself and his own mind, and that is much, but he has gained no one else. He is cautious, even secretive. He cannot lend himself to people or to causes, and he watches them pass him by while he is considering how little there is that is true. None the less, he cannot enjoy the consolations of philosophy, or religion, or of animal spirits. He speaks no more than a few lonely words about beauty. His consolation would appear to be very largely an extraordinary gift of words and the labor of arranging them and rearranging them in a poem that he calls a romance, while he considers the madness and unreason of the years through which he and his mind have passed. When he writes satire, therefore, he chooses as a center, or norm, not England as a whole, nor the Anglican Church, nor the court of Charles II; he chooses above all his own mind and his own sense of the fitness of things. War, the pretended authority of texts, the strenuous pamphleteers, the vagaries of the New Light, the venal Anglicans, the immoral Charles, are all signs of defective intelligence. He is a partisan of intelligence. "Men fell out," he wrote; "they knew not why." No other single phrase, I believe, contains so much of the meaning of Butler's satire.

As has been said, *Hudibras* was classed by its author as a romance, and since, as is clear from the context, he meant a romance in burlesque, there is no need to quarrel with so weighty an authority. The romantic classification can cause no difficulty since the story provides a lover, a lady, and the attempt of the first to win the second. The definition of what constitutes a burlesque poem, whether romantic or not, entails more difficulty. Without pausing to sort out and discuss the definitions that have previously been offered, I shall say, merely, that burlesque consists primarily, in one line of its development, in realizing an obviously and admittedly improbable action. This means that if the action is improbable it is immediately accepted by the reader without demur or debate for what it is; and it carries characters, scenes, and incidental properties equally improbable which are just as immediately accepted. Hence, burlesque is more like fantasy, or fairy stories, than it is like any other literary kind; Butler defined his poem sufficiently when he called it a romance, since to him the term meant a sequence of improbable actions.

But if *Hudibras* is a romance, it is many things besides. For one thing it is travesty; for another, it is satire; for a third, it is burlesque, a term which we must retain for the sake of our own convenience. The author's literary originality lies not so much in the sustained use of the verse form, excellently as he adapted that to his purpose, as it does in the balance which he keeps between the real and the fantastic, or burlesque, elements in his design; between the identification of historical social forces that he was satirizing and the never-never land traversed by his characters. Either one of these tasks is sufficiently difficult to challenge the ability of any first-rate writer. Swift and Byron, in achieving a union of these diverse elements, used more definite and extensive patterns of travel and adventure than did Butler, one creating entire lands and peoples for his fantasy, the other being content with a less fantastic travelogue. The ground trod by Hudibras and

Ralpho, on the other hand, is far less easily identified than either Lilliput or the Cyclades. The action of the poem is assumed to take place in England, though Butler never says that it does; the setting is vague; the properties only those of immediate use in the action. One can, indeed, say that Butler is too fond of the abstract to be able to create a rich fictional setting for his fable. But it seems more to the point to say that if *Hudibras* is first of all a romance and a fantasy, the misty background, the properties which are at hand as if by magic, are precisely appropriate to that kind of poem. In the same way, it may be true to say that *Hudibras* is structurally weak and wandering; but it is perhaps more enlightening to say that structural vagary is one of the most usual characteristics of romance. Against this indeterminate landscape we see the perfectly determinate characters; our minds are diverted, our attention is held by them. They are not real; we meet them not as people who persuade us that they have a meaning. Real people could not live and breathe and act in the hazy atmosphere of this myth; and it does not matter that they could not do so; for the author is presenting us not with single characters, but with the composite and monstrous characteristics of a period and some of its dominant attitudes.

Perhaps enough has been said to suggest what seems to me the chief determining quality of *Hudibras* as a whole— the quality of the myth, or the fantasy, or the fairy tale. Someone is sure to protest at once, however, that this unreal atmosphere cannot possibly be the most important literary quality of *Hudibras*. How can this poem be a fantasy, I imagine the questioning protest to run, when everybody knows that it is above everything else a markedly sharp and witty and timely piece of writing? Have you not yourself been at some pains to show that Butler was an intellectualist, a skeptic, a cool reasoner? And is not his best-known poem an early monument to the age of prose and reason? The main answer to such questions is a simple "yes," suggesting anew why *Hudibras* is, in the complication of its effects, one of the most amazing works ever written. It may be added, however, that Butler as a conscious literary artist, knew quite well what he was about in choosing a traditionally romantic structure to satirize both that structure and those contemporary aspects of life which seemed to him dangerously nonsensical.

Concerning the style in which the poem is built, we may find that no very fruitful discussion is possible; at the same time, so much has been written about "burlesque" verse, and the subject is of so much importance to Butler's imitators, that we cannot avoid a brief discussion of the verse form of *Hudibras*. That form is, of course, the octosyllabic or four-stress riming couplet. The form was not new; it is, in fact, one of the oldest forms of modern, as opposed to classical, poetry. I suspect that the extent to which it was the vehicle of medieval French romance formed one of the reasons why Butler was glad to adapt it to satirical uses. I imagine that his dislike of romances was owing partly to the circumstance that they were romances and partly to the unfortunate fact that so many of them were French. The verse form came across the Channel in Chaucer's time and enjoyed some popularity in English, though not predominantly for satirical purposes. In the seventeenth century, indeed, it is particularly pastoral and lyrical in mood and accent, as in William Browne and in Milton. The satirical couplets scattered through Elizabethan and Jacobean plays, the rough verse prefacing so many Civil War pamphlets, the poems of Cleaveland and those in the Musae Deliciarum, are insufficient to deprive Butler of the credit of having made this kind of verse a telling satirical instrument.

What is the difference between Milton's couplets
With wanton heed and giddy cunning

> The melting voice in mazes running
> Untwisting all the chains that tie
> The hidden soul of harmony;

and those in which Butler's Sidrophel could tell

> How many Dukes, and Earls, and Peers,
> Are in the Planetary Spheres,
> Their Airy Empire: and command
> Their sev'ral strengths by Sea and Land;
> What factions th'have, and what they drive at
> In public Vogue, and what in private.[1]

Both deal hyperbolically with matters beyond the ordinary range of events, with improbabilities, using rhetorical devices that are both elaborate and condensed. Milton's verse, however, attempts to suggest to the reader or listener another kind of sensuous and lyrical experience. It is at once emotionally soothing and emotionally disturbing. Butler on the other hand never makes the lyricist's attempt to engross the entire personality of his readers; he is active and logical rather than sensuously suggestive; impersonal rather than personal; remote rather than immediate; amusing rather than appealing. In this instance, at least, the difference between the two kinds of verse is not primarily one of the choice of words, or of movement, or even of the artistic purpose of the author. The difference is primarily a difference in men. One is capable of feeling sensuous delight and of believing that it is a good thing; he takes pleasure in that complex association of memories and of habits of observation which contributes to the sense of beauty, and he tries to satisfy his own sense of beauty by his own poetry. The other poet pays no attention to what we ordinarily mean by a sense of beauty; it does not occur to him that it is important; he feels no need to induce it in others. He takes no pains to distinguish between the beautiful and the unbeautiful, or between the moral and the immoral; he is

[1] *Hudibras,* p. 158–59.

scornfully cognizant of the thousand differences between the rational and the irrational, and he carries in stock an even greater number of modern instances of human imbecility. Given these temperamental differences in the poets, the differences in diction and in rhythm between lyrical and unlyrical octosyllabics follow simply enough and examples can easily be gathered by anyone in search of diversion.

It is necessary to distinguish the verse of *Hudibras* not only from lyrical verse but from other burlesque verse in the same meter, chiefly that of Scarron and his translators and imitators in English, and of travesty in general such as travesties of Virgil and Ovid. We have seen that *Hudibras* is itself a travesty in part, in so far as it satirizes the romantic conventions of form and content. If this were all that it did it would deserve no unique place in literary history such as it actually holds.

We can find no marked difference in verse form between, let us say, Cotton's *Virgil Travestie* and *Hudibras;* but the difference in scope and in meaning is at once apparent. The travesty is almost entirely a literary tidbit, concocted for the pleasure of educated readers thoroughly familiar with the originals. It may bear a relation to contemporary life or to a satirical presentation of it, but as we shall see in a later instance, the satirist who tries to present in a consistent way both the travesty of a classical pattern and a social satire as well, has his hands full. The travesty in *Hudibras* is an unobtrusive and incidental element; it appears as merely a part of, or as another example of, unreason and unreality. Hence, in examining the poems written after the publication of *Hudibras* and of *Scarronides*, we should be put to it to find the proper point of reference if we regarded only the form of the verse. We shall need rather to examine the content and the main drift of the later works.

The hudibrastic couplet met a formidable competitor in

the heroic couplet. The former was extremely popular and was considerably imitated for well over a century. But in its own day it failed to have so general a vogue as the couplet of Dryden. I suspect that it did not because it was not used by the dramatists, and further, that the dramatists eschewed it because of the difficulties which it puts in the way of the actor. In short passages the hudibrastic couplet is a better vehicle for pointed epigram than is the heroic. But in longer passages, both sense and sound are too often interrupted by the rime, and the temptation to parenthesis also becomes very strong. The effects of this temptation are easily seen when this verse form goes to pieces in the hands of Churchill. Furthermore, the fashionable poetic literature of the Restoration was required to be either elegant or august. *Hudibras* was neither. At its best it possesses a leanness and a hardness which comparatively few heroics achieve, and Butler did not neglect to illustrate the incurable tendency to heroic inflation in his second version of *The Elephant in the Moon*.

Nevertheless, the octosyllabic couplet is an exceedingly difficult form to control. Limited in the first place to non-dramatic uses, it is further limited by its tendency to change mood in the course of a few lines. At first sight this may appear to be a very desirable quality, suggesting the possibility of adaptation to many uses. In practice, however, dependability is just as great an asset as adaptability, and the octosyllabic couplet has shown great capacity for getting those who write it off the track. If the couplets are closed, they are exceedingly irritating in their monotony; if they are open, they are likely to be equally irritating in diffuseness and inconsequence. Butler's own jesting comment on one line for sense and one for rime is a fair indication of the dangers of the medium. For good heroics, an easy length is desirable; for hudibrastics, a hard, sensible brevity. The apparent easiness of the form has misled many

writers into attempting it, who have proved that to produce even one good couplet is a hard task indeed, while to
achieve a broad pattern is beyond them entirely.

Butler thought that a good style is like truth: it contains nothing but what is plain, open, and easy to come at
both for writer and reader. This perhaps sounds like
strange doctrine from a poet whose fame rests partly on a
supposed faculty for bringing out-of-the-way comparisons
and other figures of speech into his work. They may have
been startling to the author; they may seem startling to us.
The point is, however, that they seemed apt to him, and
most of them strike us in the very same way.

When we apply the word "hudibrastic" to other works
than *Hudibras*, we cannot limit the meaning of it to the
form of the verse. Apparently the term has meaning only
in the field of satire. It may refer to the nature of the thing
attacked, to the content of the story or fable, to the point of
view of the satirist, to the form of the verse, or to a mixture
of two or more of these elements. Although "hudibrastic"
is applied almost universally to poems written in the verse
form of *Hudibras*, without respect to the other qualities of
the poem to which it may be applied, and without respect
to the other early satirists in this form, it will not be
possible to confine the inquiry to such simple limits in discussing the imitators of Butler.

What does a writer do when he sets out to imitate
Hudibras? Obviously, imitation does not mean duplication,
for duplication is as undesirable to a writer as it is impossible to a personality. It means that one man's way of
thinking has seemed to another to be so convenient and
attractive that he thinks of himself as being in some sense
a disciple; it may mean also that aside from a sort of spiritual kinship, the follower finds his master's method of
expression so apt that he takes as much of it as he can
assimilate for his own use. The accent, the superficial

symbols of a style, are the easiest to imitate, without any intellectual connection necessarily existing between the original author and his imitator. Hence it comes about that people so diverse as Matthew Prior, the diplomatic errand boy, and Thomas Fessenden, the New England editor and Jack-of-all-trades, both claim to write, and do write, hudibrastic verse, though underneath this common claim is a world of diversity.

When we read *Hudibras* in connection with the rest of Butler's work, we are struck by the way in which his general views of society and human nature transcend the limits of his best poem, and we conclude that the author was not temperamentally or intellectually a very good or very useful partisan. His view of humanity was too consistently somber to allow him to go all the way in condemning any part of it. There seems little doubt, however, that to his contemporaries, and to those who immediately followed him, he appeared to be predominantly and especially the satirist of Dissent. His literary fame rested then, as it rests now, on what he had to say in retrospect about the forces commonly held responsible for the Civil War. None of his contemporaries praises the sinuous debates between Hudibras and the Widow, or the burlesque meeting of the Rump, or the satire on romance. But many were no doubt glad to have a lampoon on the excesses of a troublesome part of the population and to have gained thereby a convenient point of literary reference for attacking these same forces or other forces which could be shown, fairly or not, to have gained their strength from '41 and their shame from '49. *Hudibras* was assumed to be for all practical purposes an expression of High Anglicanism and of absolute royalty, and is therefore the source of, and in a sense the authority for, a great deal of intensely partisan verse by men who enjoyed no part of Butler's comparatively broad and impersonal view of the principles involved.

We can therefore distinguish several types among the imitators of *Hudibras*. First, there are those who were amused by the verse form and who experimented with it themselves, often, apparently, on the assumption that the form was easy to handle or that it would be effective even though mishandled. The second class took over the verse form, more or less of the hudibrastic machinery, and also what they conceived to be Butler's political point of view. A third class were interested not so much in the obvious marks of hudibrastic verse, or in the fable, or in the politics of Butler, as they were in the subtler qualities of his mind, such as his precision, his polish, his playfulness, and his witty and agnostic movement through the field of familiar notions.

Among the imitators those authors with the freshest and most inventive minds naturally produced the most creditable imitations. *Hudibras*, indeed, has marked shortcomings as the source and beginning of a satiric school. In the first place, it is too thorough, too complete; little is left to be said about the main defects of the Dissenting temper after Butler has gone over them.

In the next place, the poem can be said to have closed rather than to have inaugurated a period. In a sense, Butler wrote extensive, and learned, and amusing footnotes to the history of the Civil Wars and of the experiments in government that followed them. The years from 1640 to 1660 were to him a bloody, confused, and meaningless interlude; or, if the blood and confusion had any meaning, it was a warning against allowing an ignorant and passionate theocracy, an ignorant and passionate democracy, to have any part in the matters of state. Nasty and crooked as the course of government must be, that course must be shaped by sensible and shrewd men of this world, not by men claiming authority in both this world and the next. Men may be immoral, but they need not be unintelligent.

Butler's prose notes show that he felt almost as strongly in opposition to the Roman power in England, but he never got to the point of working his ideas into verse. The satirical current flowed on without him. He made no pretense to prophecy; one reads him in vain to find out what he thought would happen or what ought to happen in England. He records only his interpretation of what he has seen. To him, it is a farce so fantastic that only a burlesque can do it justice.

In other ways, too, Butler may be regarded as one who looked backward rather than forward in time. He lashes scholastic philosophy, but his allusions to Descartes and Hobbes are by no means complimentary; he spends hundreds of lines in ridiculing soothsaying and astrology, but he finds little to choose between them and the new experimental science; he decries worship of the classics and the imitation of contemporary foreign literatures, but his allusions to his own English contemporaries are few and frosty. His cultural indignations are very largely reserved for former cultures, while he feels little generosity for movements of his own day. It is as though he felt that all things had come to an end in his time. In any event, he could not turn himself into a literary handy man for any party, and that was the requirement of the age for a man of letters who wanted to get ahead.

Those among his literary followers who took over chiefly the political tendency of *Hudibras* as their satirical guide found themselves beating a dead horse. And the more they took over, the worse off they were. It is true that the "jealousies and fears" which occasioned the Civil Wars, and which the wars in turn occasioned, lived for a very long time in the national memory, as such fears will. But it seems equally true that there was no real political danger from the Independents and the Presbyterians, as such, in England after the Restoration. The members became more secular in attitude and their interests came to be identified with those of the trading and manufacturing classes. They fought for toleration, indeed, but in relation to this issue showed power only in conjunction with the Catholic interest, as in the Revolution of '88; of themselves they were not sufficiently numerous or sufficiently united on religious issues to constitute a political danger. For this reason those satires directed against religious Dissent give the impression of boxing with the shadows of ghosts. The intellectual content of *Hudibras* became attenuated to the thin cries of Tory pamphleteers who could interpret the opposition as bearing with it the seeds of '41 and of the Good Old Cause. The chief points of political satire in *Hudibras* were true enough, and well enough known, to become telling political commonplaces in a fearful and restless society.

PART TWO

POLITICAL HUDIBRASTICS

III

HUDIBRAS IN ENGLAND

SAMUEL BUTLER felt allegiance to truth; he felt, or at least he expressed, no allegiance to any party. This preference for the inclusive rather than the exclusive principle forms the first partition between *Hudibras*, considered as political satire, and those poems which were written later supposedly on the same model. Butler, in spite of his personal disapproval of Charles, seems to have been temperamentally in agreement with Clarendon's policy and with the theory that the King in his Council constituted a national government. He had found no reason to suppose that the struggle of parties for power conducted to anything but civil confusion and war. To him, party warfare meant national disruption. As we have tried to show, he reached this conclusion very largely on account of his own temper of mind, and he points his political satire quite naturally at the most powerful and most troublesome minorities, after their power had been scattered.

His followers in the mode of *Hudibras* tend to do two things, each of which is foreign to Butler's position. In the first place, they write from a strict party point of view; in the second place, they have little or nothing to add to the outlines of Butler's original caricatures. Furthermore, although they are themselves frankly party men, they insist that party politics as evidenced by the opposition, will lead again to civil war and to a new overthrow of the royal government. When such fears die down, political verse in the hudibrastic manner dies also. When those fears flare up again, we are likely to find an accompanying flare of this verse. It is directed chiefly against Presbyterianism,

Dissent, and Catholicism, particularly when the motive of rabble-rousing can be connected with their activities, and against Methodism, against revolutionary principles in America, and near the last, against the ideas of Jefferson after the Revolution in America. The dominant moods of these burlesques are contempt and fear. The assumptions behind them may be stated as follows: If religious, economic, and political minorities are allowed free play in a society, they will ruin the state. The assumption might be more nearly justified, if *change* were substituted for *ruin*, but to most of the satirists whom we shall mention, *change* and *ruin* were synonymous.

Some exceptions to the rule naturally occur. Trumbull in America, Cleland in Scotland, and Thomas Ward for the Catholics, turned the hudibrastic machinery against the Anglican and the imperial interests; Cleland and Ward because they were fighting for what they considered to be old and central conventions of their society, Trumbull because he assumed that the center of sovereignty had been shifted to this side of the Atlantic in the natural "course of human events."

In surveying the widely variant examples of hudibrastic political satire, we must come much closer to the field of contemporary controversy than Butler, as it seems to us, ever allowed himself to come. In doing so we shall look first at England, then at Scotland and Ireland, and finally, across the Atlantic, at America.

THOMAS D'URFEY AND HUDIBRASTIC VERSE, 1680–90

Thomas D'Urfey enjoyed a reputation as a jolly fellow and a song-writer and gained some popularity as a writer for the Restoration stage; but it is not difficult to agree with Day, one of his biographers, that his two hudibrastic poems, *Butler's Ghost* and *Collin's Walk*, though never reprinted are "among his happiest contributions to literature."

In *Butler's Ghost* D'Urfey wrote some such poem as Butler might have written had he turned himself into a versifying pamphleteer and written "to the times." It is a high-Tory pamphlet directed chiefly against Shaftesbury, Monmouth, Titus Oates and Slingsby Bethel. This fact, together with some others that differentiate the poem from *Hudibras* in style and method, merits some discussion.

One reason, I suspect, why *Hudibras* is a poem of unique flavor is that it is essentially retrospective. It makes no difference whether Hudibras is or is not Sir Samuel Luke, nor whether any others of the burlesque actors are ever identified with historical figures. Butler's poem is in some of its moods a satiric song of victory—an anatomy of the spiritual and political offenses of Dissent. When Butler turned from this subject he did not become an active party satirist; rather he wrote about general and abstract subjects. One might infer from Butler that Dissent and Presbyterianism had been wiped out in 1660.

The fact was, of course, that however English Presbyterianism had been shattered as a coherent political body by the Restoration and however it had been secularized by time and by the pressure of events thereafter, the remnants constituted, as minorities will, at once a party strength and a party hazard. It is probable, also, that the word *Presbyterian* like the word *Catholic* was far more terrifying in its political connotations than any actual body of persons of either sect could have been at the time at which *Butler's Ghost* was written. Hence the poem is anything but retrospective and playful and philosophical. It attacks Shaftesbury's political tenets and ambitions by linking the actual fears of the Tories in 1680 with the remembered fears of the Royalist party in 1641.

This joining of the battle cries of two historical eras obviously complicates the problem of the satirist. D'Urfey simplifies this problem and solves it for his purpose by adopting the machinery and in good part the theory and the manner of the Restoration farce comedy. He makes the outlandish figure of the original Hudibras change under our eyes to the figure of a calculating Restoration beau, and with great economy shows us through this transformation both the flow of the "country" interest into the "city" interest and an extreme example of the change from the unlovely but stern Presbyterian crusader to the dulcet but worldly Presbyterian man about town.

As pointed and specific social satire this goes beyond anything that Butler attempted, and there is also scarcely any better example of the adaptation of the hudibrastic machinery by means of fashionable literary methods. The influence of dramatic figures and satire is obvious in D'Urfey's poem. Hudibras is the countryman who learns the sins of the city, Ralpho is the pimp, and the Whig leaders are the fashionable and venal men about town.

The design of the poem is clear. As the poem begins, Hudibras is about to commit suicide on having failed to win the hand of the widow, a Tory. Ralpho dissuades him, pointing out that he has failed because his manners and dress are uncouth and because he has not used bribery. Hudibras listens to reason, has his face smooth shaven, orders a new suit, bribes the two Whigs who are the trustees of the widow's estate, and thereupon easily wins the lady. The trustees are the more happy to agree to this settlement since each has committed fornication with the heroine and she is about to give birth to a "young moon-calf Whigg."

Hudibras celebrates the betrothal with a dinner attended by Whig leaders and one Tory "Proto," a friend of the bride. The dinner develops into a brawl after Pygmy (Shaftesbury) has been told that the abetters of his career and designs are the devil, Cromwell, Bradshaw, and Hugh Peters.

Hudibras is not an important figure in this second half of the poem. He is busy seeing that the dinner is served and is then told by Ralpho that his bride has left the table and is even then being ravished in another room by Stalliano (Bethel). Hudibras tries to argue that this cannot be true, but he sees, is convinced, and after a struggle ties the bride's hands with her garter, trusses Stalliano with a cord, and shuts them in separate rooms. For his part, he is overcome with grief and "curses Fatal Love and Marriage."

The persons satirized in the poem are Monmouth (Publicola), Shaftesbury (Pygmy), Sunderland (Sodom), Pilkington (Pimpino), Shute (Backoso), and Slingsby Bethel and Titus Oates (Stalliano and Doctoro). These last appear of course as Shimei and Corah in *Absalom and Achitophel*. Also the author refers to a "squab thing," probably Algernon Sidney, and to a "sniveling cur," by whom it seems likely he means Sir Patience Ward. At least we meet the same epithet in a later hudibrastic satire where the latter is called "That sniffling whig-mayor, Patience Ward."[1] Probably no historical figures are indicated by Hudibras and Ralpho. Their story rather serves as a frame into which the Whig leaders are set. The idea of the dinner party may have been suggested to D'Urfey partly by the dinner given by Pilkington in March, 1682, after Shaftesbury had been set free. We know at least that the same men appear in this satire who were present at that time.

In introducing Stalliano the author gives the main antipathies of the Whigs, the "Pope, and French, and K(*ing*) and D(*uke*)." He has no doubts about the essential spirit of the Whig movement; Stalliano's color, he says, is

> Old Forty One Fanatick Blew;
> Tho modern Statists now are seen,
> To change the Colour into Green;

a reference, of course, to Shafestbury's Green Ribbon Club.

[1] Thomas Ward, *England's Reformation*.

The chief charge against Stalliano is the use of his office as sheriff for party ends and for enriching himself at the same time.

Doctoro's sins are those of pride, and lying, and of using religious passions for the benefit of the Whigs. The other characters are blamed for personal greed and for party interest, but Shaftesbury naturally gets most of the attention. The theory and practice of the Whigs of 1682 as put into his mouth are somewhat as follows:

Nothing can be gained except by time, policy and patience. A commonwealth is as hard to achieve as the restoration of Charles II was, but the "Conscientious Men" will be able to overturn the monarchy once more if the party "minds its hits." Violence will not do. It is true of course that in 1648 "Religion was the Sword"; but at that time the rebel party was in power, whereas in 1682 they were not. Hence they must "grace their Plots with subtlety." Wit, not force, is the weapon now. Publicity, rumor, whispering campaigns and "All things that can the King perplex . . . To urge him to strike first," are to be employed. And no better means can be found of stirring discontent and fear "Than th' old Authentick sham Religion."

As for himself, his career has been distinguished by zeal for the state; and he deserted the King's cause in 1644 for the sake of conscience. He denies the Tory charges that ambition, ingratitude and an eye for the main chance have been his chief guides in politics.

Leaving aside the question of Shaftesbury's personal character, we see how the author, although of course disapproving of them, gives a fair picture of party aims and methods through his statement of the Whig designs. The saints are not now militant; the minority church party is becoming an increasingly secular party; it hopes to organize permanent obstruction and opposition to the royal interest; it will use any politic means to gain popular support and to embarrass its opponents. And it will be assured of the cohesion of its leading spirits through the perquisites and corruptions of political office.

From Butler's satire we gain a view of Dissent as something so infinitely divisive that at last each man stands alone impregnable in his own peculiarities. D'Urfey on the other hand sees how Dissent can be gathered into groups and fostered and used as a constant political weapon. Butler was right. And D'Urfey was right also. But the latter happened to strike at an aspect of Dissent which has become increasingly important—the organization and emotional motivation of minorities.

In tone the poem is suave, pleasant, at times almost gay in spite of the necessary burlesque action and the incisiveness of the political satire. The author has the gift of phrase, of which the best example is the picture of

> the Squires gloomy beard
> Wet with the Argumental froth.

He also has a good sense for humorous situations and actions, as when he causes Hudibras to save his life through being unable to decide whether to fall on his sword or to hang himself. He is considerably less skillful in handling abstract ideas and very sensibly does not often attempt to do so.

D'Urfey's *Collin's Walk*, published in 1690 and dedicated to the Earl of Danby, satirizes two attitudes toward the revolutionary settlement, namely that of the Presbyterians and that of the discontented Anglicans. His preface is explicit. He wishes, he says, to expose "the Humors of a Grumbling Church of England-Man, and an opinionated Presbyter . . . my sole Business being to rally my Country-Men into Union and good Humor." His language is, I fear, too harsh to have done much toward national union, but in any event he carries out as well as he can his other intention: "to publish the Regard and Honour I have for the Established Church, by explaining the Envy, Errors, Stubbornness and Foppery of her two implacable Enemies, Popery and Presbytery." In fact the poem is a very good indication of how, after the Restoration, Catholicism joined the sects as another form of dissent from the Establishment, and how far distant even in 1690 the efforts of the latitudinarians still were from achieving "comprehension." It reminds one also of the difficulty men felt in thinking of any problem in the church in terms other than national or antinational. D'Urfey in his preface chides the common people for grumbling at those taxes "which must of necessity follow so great an Affair, as the restoring our Church to her Ancient Priviledges and Rights." The temper of this clause makes it easy to credit the quotation in Burnet to the effect that three-fourths of the ordinary business of the government had to do with the settlement of religion. It is perhaps significant also that the scene in *Collin's Walk* opens in the country and shifts to London exactly as in *Butler's Ghost*. The likeness suggests that D'Urfey was most concerned about the political aberrations of the country interest.

Although *Collin's Walk* is more complex in theme than the earlier poem, it is quite as clear and simple in structure. The main action goes as follows: The Major calls on Collin, his tenant, while he is working in his barn, in order to convert him to the Jacobite cause. They retire to Collin's house to drink beer and to carry on the discussion. The Major fails in his purpose but offers to pay the cost of a trip to London, where he is sure Collin will be won over to his side by "Crowds of Priests, in Parson's Gowns" and by signs of popular discontent with the government. Collin agrees to go, since in any case he wishes to collect twenty pounds owed him for hay by a dealer in the city. The "walk" begins in the second canto. The couple go through

Temple Bar to St. Dunstans and the Old Exchange and witness a Lord Mayor's parade. Collin sits on the Major's shoulder to get a better view but falls when a squib goes off at his ear. The Major fights the offender and both are saved and jailed and finally freed by the constable. The officer is sympathetic, for though he now keeps an alehouse he was himself formerly a major in the Civil Wars. The first day ends thus with Collin twitting the Major on how little he had so far seen of any grumblers or any "Cabal of Popish frolick."

On the next day the odd couple go to Westminster to visit Parliament. There they listen to complaints against taxation, until they are frightened away by the report that a mob of 40,000 people is converging on the House to protest against an embargo on silk. They retire to the house of one of the Major's friends, a quack doctor, who is concealing his brother, a Jesuit, disguised as his sister. The "sister" and Collin begin a debate which develops into a series of insults until the "sister" is sent from the room and Collin rushes away in anger.

The next night Collin is in better spirits since he has received his twenty pounds that morning, and he and the Major attend the play, *Bartholomew Fair*, where Collin wins the applause of the house through the familiar farcical device of regarding the action on the stage as real. The presence of *Zeal of the Land Busy* convinces him that he must be present at a conventicle. Accordingly, when the "Rabbi" is about to be put in the stocks he draws his sword and leaps to the stage. He is clubbed down but rises to prove that he is a man of consequence by showing his gold. On this a woman appears and leads him away.

They go to an alehouse. The drink Collin buys being too small, she throws the pot at his head. He apologizes; he has not before known a Sister who drank wine, and in such quantity as she requires. She next tries to convince him that it is customary for men to treat ladies, but he insists that none of the Brothers has ever thought treating anything but "senseless."

Thereupon his partner says that she was only testing his steadfastness. She doesn't want luxury; his very appearance is a breakfast to her. They agree to go to bed and she retires supposedly to make ready. But she has stolen his money while at the table and sends back a note to say so. Meanwhile the Major has traced him and has witnessed the whole scene from a closet. He now scorches Collin for hypocrisy with the "Aqua Fortis of ill language." Collin, however, says it was all on account of predestination; his ill fortune had been foretold by a gypsy when he was a boy. The Sister must have received her mercenary nature through having been begot by a priest on a "Female Whig." He concludes that if free will had been operative "Purse had been here, and I not mist it," that he will lose his reputation among the Saints for having been found out, and that the town is not for him.

In the pattern of this story, again, D'Urfey's ability to handle material dramatically is clear. His bias is also equally clear. For in the third canto or "act" the Major is converted to thoroughgoing Anglicanism by the extravagances which the author puts into the mouth of the Jesuit, while Collin remains unconverted to the end.

This result is, however, true to Collin's character throughout, and both his character and position are not only consistent but interesting. Physically he is, like Hudibras and his long line of spiritual children, unprepossessing. He is the son of a preacher. He is almost a dwarf, is splayfooted, full-bearded, and has lost one eye at hurling. Ordinarily he wears clothes patched in many colors, but on the Sabbath or at a fair "Would blaze in Manufacture Grey."

His father, however, had apparently taught him to

read and to argue. He has been by turns an Anglican, a Quaker, and a Dissenter according to his interest, but politically he is much more satisfactory than the Major is. He insists that

> I am for Union in the Main
> What ere opinion I maintain

and that he is, on the whole, a better friend to the Establishment than the Major. For Collin tells always a "plain an open Tale" against Popery, while the Major, though a professing Anglican, not only voices his real disaffection "in grumbling clubs" but is trying to get Collin to join him.

The interior of Collin's house, although not described with any special satiric intention, deserves some notice because it shows the care with which the author provides consistent background for his characters and how the descriptive passages enliven the poem as a whole.

> The story of the Prodigal,
> Instead of Arras, deck'd the Wall:
> With Proclamations mix'd, and Votes:
> The Suffering Phiz of Righteous O—:
> Jenkins and Naylors Exhortations:
> And Grizzels Ode, so fam'd for Patience;
> The thrifty owner did invent
> For cheap and comely Ornament.

The author succeeds in making a great deal of fun of Collin as a country lout in town, but in his own setting he is anything but an unattractive figure.

The poem as a whole, as a literary production, is firm in structure. The verse form is handled deftly and the descriptive passages are compact and engaging. Although there seems to be no personal satire intended, D'Urfey has succeeded very well in placing emphasis on the issues he is presenting by commanding the interest of the reader in the burlesque characters and their actions.

Followers of D'Urfey

A good many poems following D'Urfey in content, point of view, and treatment, were published in the decade following 1680.

"The Privilege of Our Saints" is a publication which owes to Butler everything but its title. Apparently as part of the attack on the Whigs, the publisher of this broadside excerpted parts of the debate in *Hudibras* Part II, Canto II, on whether it is obligatory for a Saint to observe oaths once taken. The cutting was done judiciously and all references to the story of Hudibras and to dead political issues, such as the Solemn League and Covenant, are excised.

The several broadsides in hudibrastic verse against Charles II and Titus Oates, though slight, have some effectiveness within their range. The "Parallel betwixt Popery and Phanaticism" is written chiefly in heroic couplets but begins with octosyllabics on Oates. It is interesting chiefly because it emphasizes the charge that both Catholicism and the sects intended to subvert the governemnt by violent means. "Funeral Tears upon the Death of Captain William Bedloe" is an ironic poem linking Oates and Bedloe and imploring the latter to swear himself back to life to continue the work of saving his country from the Jesuits. "Epipapresbyter", wittily phrased, plays on the number of causes which Oates had been allied with—"Proteus Lodges in his Face." "The Panegyrick upon Oates" turns on a pun. Oats are the most healthful grain in England, and the author hopes that "Oates of such known Divinity" will be exposed in some "sacred Press" or hung up to "raise our Contemplation."

The brief "Whigs Address" humbly begs Charles to fill his ministry with Whigs with the threat that if he does not he will learn "by sad Disasters, That you are Lord, yet we are Masters." The poem also reiterates the familiar charge of using religion for party ends.

> For tho' Religion bears the name,
> It's Government is all our Aim.

"On the Dissolution" is a savage and patriotic satire against the Duchess of Portsmouth and Charles. He is "Ruling by Letchery not Law"; his "Government is a Disease Made up of Vice and Sensual Ease," and he reigns not according to English but to French law.

The first, second and third collections of anti-Catholic and anti-Jacobite poems, all published in 1689, contain a number of poems in burlesque verse related to that of *Hudibras*.

Dryden and King James receive attention in the "Humble Address." The laureate is made to say that only two people in the kingdom will resist the king's power of dispensation, and these he will "Rhyme . . . into better manners" with Part II of the "Hind and the Panther." For the rest the author hopes that they will sacrifice "Their stubborn Consciences to yours" and that the King's

> Judges too will over-awe,
> The poor dead Letter of the Law.

This poem is but one of a number in burlesque verse in which Catholicism takes the place of Presbyterianism as the archenemy of traditional English liberties.

"The Converts" attacks some of those "That change their Faith to please their King," notably the Earls of Peterborough, Salisbury and Sunderland, and Sir Edward Hales.

"The Audience" presents James as an infant to whom the ambassador from Rome flings "The consecrated Robe and Clout," and to whom Tyrconnel is special nurse.

In the "Dialogue" between James and his wife she complains that

> Your spurious Issue grow and thrive;
> While mine are dead ere well alive,

and that she is blamed for his faults. He reproves her for

favoring the union of the Catholic and Dissenting interests, for the Dissenters are too wise to be caught by the promise of free consciences for all; they suspect that the Catholics will ultimately have the best of the bargain.

In "A Dialogue between Father Peters and the Devil," the Devil reproves the priest for having used too much force in proselytizing; the English must be convinced of a cause before they will truly adhere to it. His own fate is what he must have long foreseen, and the fate of England is determined by the successes of William.

"Hounslow Heath," an ironic poem against James, praises him for

> His Faith, his Zeal, his Constancy,
> Aversion to all Bigotry,

his courage, his unwillingness to use force, and his impartial justice. The author wishes that Dryden might be hanged for having written the "Hind and the Panther."

Turning again to the more considerable productions, we find a poem "In Vindication of the Late Publick Proceedings" and an extensive satire on Roger L'Estrange called *Pendragon, or the Carpet Knight*.

The title page of the "Vindication" carries a quotation from *Hudibras* to the effect that when a tyrant invades the liberties of a nation, he uses the laws to defend his usurpation. The poem is written in octosyllabics, sober rather than burlesque in tone, and it commands our interest here chiefly because of the parallel implied between the Jacobites and the sectaries whom Butler attacked. The Tory takes the position that all are bound in loyalty to support James, and to rely on the promises that he might make if he should return. The Trimmer is not willing to run this risk and says that no oath of loyalty is binding on a nation if keeping that oath requires the nation to destroy itself. He asks,

> Shall we in earnest entertain
> Boundless Prerogative again?
> Or shall we still resist, that you
> May safe be, and seem loyal too?

The same general political point of view is represented by *Pendragon*. The poem is called a "Kalendar" only because it is arranged in twelve cantos. The characters are the Knight Pendragon; his squire Hugh, or Hugo; Laurence, a curate; Serena, a lady; and her maid, Thomasine. The plot is simple; it concerns Pendragon's suit for the hand of Serena who marries a rich citizen instead. As subplot we have the affair between Laurence and Thomasine who ultimately marry. It is scarcely necessary to detail the steps in a plot so conventional.

The poem is very neatly put together, but as satire it combines savagery and indecency to an unusual degree. The author declares in the preface that he is attacking "Factions and Perswasions"; but the most vigorous and extensive portions of the poem taunt L'Estrange with physical impotence—and he was eighty-two years old when the poem was published. Hence the early cantos, that attack the defects of the man's opinions rather than those of his body, are the most telling. L'Estrange is charged with Catholic sympathies and with condemning the Reformation by implication. In debate with the curate Laurence who is a Romanist, L'Estrange is made to insist that he never said explicitly that the Reformation was a "Scandal to the Nation." Laurence agrees but declares that the inference is clear. The author adds that visions of power had deceived the Dissenting interest into a league with the Catholic.

> The Thoughts of riding in the Saddle
> Make weak Dissenter's Brains turn addle;
> He could not see (he grew so blind)
> The Jesuit getting up behind;
> Who soon with unexpected Flirt
> Would throw his Worship in the Dirt.

The author is at his best in passages of this sort, which are too few. The distasteful part of the poem is occasioned by a movement in the plot. Pendragon is refused by Selena and shortly thereafter receives at his home a package and an anonymous letter, both of which have been sent by his lady. The package contains a halter and the letter consists of the reasons why he should use the halter to hang himself.

The reasons are first that though he can still debauch women by the "Fop doodle" of his wit, he is too impotent to debauch them physically. Secondly, if he continues to live he will be further embroiled. Thirdly, he deserves such punishment in spite of the fact that his offenses do not come under the penal code. Next, he will be harshly dealt with in the coming revolution, and he should "Truss up yourself for good and all" instead of waiting to be mauled like Hudibras. Lastly, his writings have led his followers into errors for which they were hanged at Tyburn, so that in fairness he can do no less than commit suicide. When he is dead his body will be buried in the highway with a stake driven through his navel.

Pendragon, after reading the letter, resolves to "walk no more among the Hens," but he feels safe in the protection of the army and of the king's judges who control the laws.

When William's fleet approaches, however, he is terrified into disguising himself as a translator. Of the other characters, the curate flees to Europe despairing of the Catholic cause; Hugo goes over to William; and Selena seeks, by marrying a rich Whig merchant of London, what security she can find.

The poem can be praised for singleness of aim, for the force and variety of the verse, and for some admirable anti-Jacobite satire. The author had apparently read *Hudibras* with full understanding of everything in it but the fanciful portions of the burlesque. He goes on the assumption that we have met with several times, that the Jacobite interest in the 1680's was analogous to the dissenting interest during the Civil Wars.

The author's notion of burlesque verse is given in his preface and the connection of his satire with Butler's requires quotation:

I would rather here speak of the Laws of Burlesque, (if I knew any it had:) It stands indeed upon Four Feet: but its Liberties and Privileges are unbounded; and those Four Feet are, I think, by no means oblig'd to be but Eight Syllables; for in place of the Last, it is part of its Excellency sometimes to have Two, Three, or Four Syllables (Like so many Claws) crowded into the Time of One Foot. The Duple and Triple Rhyme, in some other Poetry much blamable, are Beauties in this: And Burlesque esteems it no Fault, for Ryme's sake, to borrow from any Language whatsoever. . . .

It is wonderful to traverse its Arbitrary Power, how it proceeds without regard to Periods, Colons, or Commas: How sometimes it will change Accents for the sake of Rhyme, and, according to the most vulgar and careless Pronunciation, leave out what Consonants it pleases. It will end the verse with a Preposition, and make Interjections at its own Libitum. . . . Sometimes it goes on with a long Bead–row of Monosyllables together, and esteems it no Blemish; at another time, one single Word, or two at most, shall compose the whole Line. Endless it would indeed be to recount its various qualifications and wild Vagaries, or to say how many different things it is like. . . .

If the Author of Hudibras had a right or took a liberty to ridicule particular Factions and Perswasions, as he thought them Faulty, sure another Man must needs have the same Privilege to expose those who are apparently mischievous to Society, and destructive to good Establish'd Government. Though I doubt whether any Man will arise with so transcendent a Genius and happy Talent for this purpose, as Mr. Butler; and great pity it was, as well as Shame, that in one respect he was suffer'd to fall so low at the last.

In closing the discussion of this extremely various material, it is appropriate to notice Dixon's *Canidia*. This is a vast poem of 580 pages, confused in object and in manner; it seems to be written in order to name all possible sources of evil. Canidia is the "Great General" of the witches who are always at work in every part of the world. The poem opens with iambic and trochaic octosyllabic couplets in groups of eight, but it breaks out into a great variety of other measures. The passage on the Civil Wars suggests in diction and in movement that the author had read *Hudibras:*

> O, what a Chaos, what a Hell
> For Twenty years, no Tongue can tell?
> Jealousies and Fears, those dismal Notes,
> Brought us all to Cutting a Throats.
> Kings-Lands, Church-Lands, all went down,
> Wide Throats swallow'd Mitre and Crown.
> The men in Steel got all the Gold,
> And all the Power, if it would hold.

Concerning his own times, Dixon exclaims "None but a Witch can paint this Age," and one who has read the satiric blasts and counterblasts of the period cannot help agreeing with him. Not the number of parties, but the shades of opinion in each; not the number of arresting personalities so much as the intertwining of policies in each man's mind make the history of the time tortuous to follow and difficult to realize. They, "quicksilver like, elude our pains." With reference to the satiric followers of Butler from 1680, however, it is possible to make a few generalizations. They assume to appeal to the national interest, whether they are opposing royal prerogative, or the Whigs, or the Catholics. Secondly, the fear of Catholicism has in general taken the place of fear of the sects, but it is felt to carry with it the same ills which the Civil War had brought. Lastly, hudibrastic verse is handled by these writers with considerable skill, but the effect of the verse is considerably modified by the influence of dramatic forms and the use of direct personal satire.

In the next part of this book we shall notice how the burlesque manner became adapted to various uses by the first decade of the eighteenth century. Here we must remark a change in the point of hudibrastic satire in England after the turn of the century, as exemplified in the poems of Edward Ward. We can see a cycle, not only in the style but in subject matter. Butler began it by satirizing Dissent and Presbyterianism as the extreme madnesses of a normally mad existence; his immediate followers took the hint by satirizing their opponents as the insane members of a normally sane society. Ward, however, cannot clearly define what the opposition is. It is many-headed, many-named; it is "Fanaticks, Dissenters, Moderators, Whigs, Low-Church-men, Saints, Reformers, or whatsoever new Denomination they are pleas'd to rank themselves under."[2] He is not a man of much logical precision, nor a man of ideas; he is a High-Church Tory of humble origin. This fact, together with the increasing ferment of parties, is enough to make him write thousands of pages in all against the forces working to undermine church and state as he loves to think of them.

His point of view is, perhaps, best expressed in *Vulgus Britannicus*, published in London in 1710. This poem is dedicated, as the title implies, to the party, or rather the class, which he designates with a mock bow as "Our Soverign Lord, the Mob," or "Our New Soverign Lord, the Rabble." At the date of this poem the more intense contentions of religion had receded, and only by allusion does Ward touch upon the religious implications of inner light. The poem is directed against the importunities and the futilities of civic inner light as represented by the unruly mob. One of the neatest things, however, about the First Book of *Vulgus Britannicus* is the point that the Mob, so long used by the Dissenters, the Whigs and

[2] *Hudibras Redivivus*. An Apology Added to the Second Edition. 1708.

the Middle-Churchmen for political ends, at last turns upon its original master, guts the Church, and burns the pews and pulpits, for no particular reason except that it is the whim of the crowd. This is practically the only action that takes place within eight hundred lines of verse, a fact which indicates the author's predominantly rhetorical manner.

Temperamentally emotional, our author is the more stirred because of the shifting face of the forces he is attacking. Which is the nation's worst enemy, the Dissenter, the Low-Churchman, the Whig, or is it all of them together bound into a shapeless social bundle? This lack of clarity in the object constitutes the weakness and the strength of Ward's satire for, had he known more, he would not have been so fearful, and, had he not been so fearful, he would not have written with that occasional energy which, when least expected, brings his poems to life.

This change in the nature of the object practically brought hudibrastic political satire to an end in England. Meston was still to write his anti-Presbyterian lines, but when he did so he was merely reviving an old issue. The Methodists awoke some of the old arguments, it is true, but only the Catholic attack was made by a practiced hand. The able men of letters were not cultivating the hudibrastic garden, and the state of politics was in general not such as to arouse the old battle cries which make up so much of the body of this sort of satire.

IV

HUDIBRAS IN SCOTLAND

ENGLISH Presbyterianism was a derivative product, and its Scotch original retained a tough and infinitely troublesome life after the English party had lost its militant character. Again, Presbyterianism in the Lowlands was the accustomed and traditional religious form of the mass of the people. Hence the Anglican bishops had always been the oppressors, the innovators, the disturbers of the peace. And it is therefore not surprising to find at least one Scotch satirist regarding in the same light the emissaries of the English court and the shaggy barbarians from the Highlands. Both are invading the "establishment."

Nevertheless, we should not forget that almost all Scots, whether Catholic, Anglican, or Presbyterian, were strongly royalist in their sympathies at different times, their temper varying in accordance with the opportunies they saw of establishing one religious form and one only throughout the country. As matters turned out at the Restoration, the Anglican hierarchy got the upper hand and held it for many years. The conditions of the victory left ambitious Presbyterians in a tight place. If they aspired to a career in politics or the professions, they must conform to the newly established Anglican communion. To escape the political witch-hunters a great many did conform, among them apparently, the first author whose work we shall examine.

Samuel Colville, author of *The Whiggs Supplication*, was born about 1640 and died about 1680, the exact dates being unknown. He was the third and youngest son of John Colville of Comrie, a chief elder, and of Elizabeth Melville of Halhill. He attended St. Andrews and wrote two books, one of them the subject of the present discussion, and but little else is known of him. There seems to be no reason, however, for rejecting or disbelieving the autobiographical references in Canto II of the *Supplication*. Presbyterianism, he says, is the faith

> Which I of late so much adored,
> But now, when I get nothing for it,
> Make me, O Muse! to change my Note,
> Declare against it, turn my Coat.

The author, since he was brought up in the home of a chief elder, was no doubt thoroughly drilled in the teachings of the Kirk. And it is quite as reasonable to suppose that his boyhood beliefs were changed after the Restoration and that he turned to episcopacy with either real or professed relief.

Although the *Supplication* was not published until just about the time of the author's death, it seems to refer to a period about fifteen years earlier. For the Squire travels to London after the time of a heavy frost and when he arrives sees the ruins left by the fire. Also some of the Whigs mentioned in the poem gather

> with a Lochaber Axe
> Resolv'd to give Dalzel his Paiks.

Colonel Dalziel was most active against the Whigs in the winter of 1666–67. Hence, since the meeting of the Whigs is said to take place in December, the poem may refer to some rallying of their forces soon after their defeat by Dalziel at Rullion Green in November. I have not, however, been able to find a trace of any actual public meeting nor any actual supplication addressed to the King. It seems likely that the main object of the poem is to satirize various points of view within the Whig or Covenanting party.

The hero of the poem is Good-man. He is attended by a Lady, a Squire, a Steed, a Dog, and a Pidgeon. He is leader of the Whigs, who are meeting to pass on a declaration or supplication to the king. The Good-man reads the petition; he and the Squire debate who shall carry it to the king. It is decided that the Squire shall go.

The Squire sets out for London, arriving while the city is still in ruins from the great fire. He meets a multitude, some in coaches, some on foot, who, he at first thinks, have come out to welcome him and bring him to the king. They examine his outfit and ask his business so persistently that he loses his temper. They are about to assault him, but are restrained by a member of the crowd, and leave the Squire unharmed. He plucks up courage and asks them not to go because he has no quarrel really with anyone "but Ralph the Squire of Sanderson." But he said this only after he thought the mob safely away. But Ralph hears and returns to battle. The Squire draws his sword, but hesitates to fight; instead he proposes to talk, whereupon Ralpho himself is much relieved. They take up the debate from *Hudibras:*

> That Synod-members, and Church-wardens
> Are Bears, and Synods are Bear-Gardens.

Ralpho's arguments in the affirmative are all quoted from Butler. The debate over, the assembly discusses indecisively who won. Then the Squire proceeds without hindrance to the king. The courtiers laugh at his looks (he thinks with approval); he leaves the court and the town and addresses a eulogy to it as he goes.

The conditions about which the Whigs complained were, indeed, severe enough. In "settling" the Scottish Church, Charles II did not pause to get the support of the General Assembly. By the Act Rescissory of 1662 all laws passed since 1633 were declared of no effect; and bishops were replaced as permanent moderators of the synods. Thus episcopacy was superimposed on presbytery as before the Civil War, but the result was reached without the consent of the Kirk having been asked. Probably by this means the enthusiasm of many Presbyterian Royalists in Scotland was dampened. Certainly many able men were driven from the Kirk. The laity were in as bad case, for Presbyterians—confessed Covenanters—had no civil standing. They were fined for nonattendance at established churches and liable to arrest if they attended conventicles. The governmental measure debated in the *Supplication* was passed by Parliament in 1662. It is known generally as the Declaration, and decreed that the Solemn League and Covenant was not binding and that it was unlawful to take up arms against the king.

The Whigs declare that they will not sign this Declaration, but they again plead their cause to the king. They remind him that they are loyal subjects in all matters in which conscience is not tampered with. Not only are they now loyal, but they supported His Majesty when his fortunes were at their lowest. While under Cromwell, some Scots supported the Protector in the hope of gain, and while during the same period "hierling" preachers omitted to pray for the king, in order to protect their livings, the covenanters were steadfast.

> But we, in the Usurpers Faces,
> Remembered you in Prayers and Graces;
> And if we had had Guns and Swords,
> Our Actions would have back'd our words.
> Our Fault, Sir, was, for which we moan,
> We thought to do it all alone.
> Since it was only want of Wit,
> Since it was a Distraction Fit,
> We pray you, Sir, be no despiser
> Of us, whom God has made no wiser.

The party has not, in the ordinary sense, used its wits; as a matter of principle it had been doggedly loyal. Now all the Whigs have to show for their consistent principles is persecution. They have had to sell their property, even their Bibles, to raise the money to pay the fines imposed on them. When all property and hope were gone, they took to arms. But they had better have stayed at home, for some were killed, and some hanged at assizes and their heads stuck up on public view. The hunted survivors were scarcely happier, for they were forced into hiding and starvation and scattered among the bogs. Now the party reaffirms its affection for royalty and pleads to be no longer despised and harried.

Thus far the supplication itself. The allusion to armed resistance shows quite clearly, I think, that the author had in mind the Whig position after the Pentland Rising in 1666. It is interesting to note that although the Whigs claim quite justly that they have long supported Charles, they leave out the historical fact that they supported him chiefly because they hoped to find in him a king who would enforce a national religion on the Presbyterian model.

Once the supplication has been read, it is debated by Good-man and the Squire. The debate brings out two characteristic political attitudes and also hints that the poem is at least in part a satire on Archbishop Sharp and Lauderdale.

The Squire's position is easy to define. He does not like the petition because it does not request the renewal of the Covenant. He is a bitter-ender and his main office in the first canto is to bring out the religious and political deficiencies of Good-man.

Good-man, for his part, believes that it would be "base" to ask the king to renew the Covenant; for that would obviously be against his conscience. As long as they are free of the Declaration, he wants to meddle no more with the government of the church. He is partly cynical, partly skeptical in his attitude. Bishops, he says, were ejected formerly, but "two or three" people still ran church affairs. Furthermore, who knows which way of government is true?

> I tell thee Fool, I think Government
> Of Church, a thing of small concernment:
> The Truth 'tis very hard to find . . .
> And since the truth is found by none,
> No more than is that turn Gold Stone,
> It's best, Zancho, for ought I see,
> To take a Pint and then agree.
> Let man have Bishops at their Ease
> And hear what Preachers best them please.

Hence Good-man will willingly say "My Lord and Grace" to bishops rather than disturb the peace. He is willing to kneel, to allow confirmation, to say amen, to wear surplice and sleeves; and

> Yea, ere his Majesty be wroth,
> I'le Primate be, and Chancellor both.

This stand by Good-man means, of course, practical desertion of the Whig cause altogether and lays him open to a fierce attack from the Squire.

Good-man, so the Squire charges, was once a hot Whig. He was keen against the Engagers and against Bishops and swore that if he ever swerved from his belief he would be a knave. Yet he changed sides in only twenty days. Why? Because he loved money and place and hoped to gain both. He is so lacking in principle that if the Covenant were again in force he would again fight the bishops —for 1,000 marks a year. Anyone who takes the Covenant and breaks it against his light is a knave;

> On singulars we will not harp,
> For the apply will be to *Sharp*.

Even though he has been corrupted, however, he need not suppose that he has the confidence of his new friends, the Cavaliers; for they will always suspect him to be what he formerly was, an archrebel.

One is tempted to believe that all these charges are a

direct attack on James Sharp. For Sharp, an able though not an extreme Presbyterian, was sent to represent the Kirk at the court of Charles both in Holland and in England. At the same time he protected his own interests so well that on the reestablishment of episcopacy he became primate of Scotland and hankered to become Chancellor as well. I can, however, find no record of his activity on behalf of the Engagers nor of a book called *Advice in Season*, concerning which the Squire twits Good-man. Good-man protests that the book is much esteemed abroad. So it is, the Squire rejoins—as a jest book. I infer that Sharp's record goes to make up part of a composite portrait, and that the author's intention is to describe the attitude taken after the Restoration by many men who had no attachment by principle or sentiment to the Covenant or any other method of control, and who, through avarice or the lack or any feeling that their salvation would depend on their choice of church government, chose the quickest way to safety and to personal advancement. In any event, the first part of the *Supplication* gives a clear notion of the positions taken by the hot and by the cold Covenanters in a time of stress.

The second part of the poem is not so satisfactory. Perhaps the author's purpose is to show that even so enthusiastic a Whig as the Squire is overcome by the splendor of Whitehall, so that instead of presenting the petition he can only assure Charles that his Scottish subjects are loyal. The chief interest lies in the burlesque description of the Squire and of his action in front of the city crowd.

It should be added, however, that the Squire when he arrives wants to see not only Ralpho, but "Sanderson." As it happens, Sanderson isn't present, possibly for the very good reason that he died some years before the Squire arrived. At least this is the right conclusion if by Sanderson is meant the Bishop of Lincoln. He died in 1662, but in 1661 his book, *Episcopacy*, had been published. The arguments advanced in this book are that bishops work according to divine and to royal law, for they follow the explicit laws of the New Testament in preaching and in administering sacraments; they also follow the laws of the Established Church which are in turn derived from practices that seem to have been approved by the early church, and which have been given the force of law by the king. The second argument is that though bishops do indeed transact ecclesiastical business in their own names, the right to do this is derived from the throne; hence the more the bishops exercise this derived power, the greater glory will be reflected on the king. In view of the anti-Erastian and anti-Episcopal principles of the Squire, he may very likely have wanted at least a brief sparring match with the bishop.

Colville's poem is not firmly made, the object of his satire is not always clear, his verse is likely to stumble, and he uses sections of *Hudibras* without giving credit in order to spin out his pages. These are serious defects. Yet the author handles the debate pointedly.

In contrast to *Hudibras*, the *Supplication* contains two elements that are utterly foreign—a jesting but entirely human sympathy with the burlesque characters, and an intimate autobiographical note. Butler writes with no trace of pity for the people of his comedy, and he writes remotely and impersonally. Furthermore, he has arrived at his own impregnable intellectual position; he may not find it altogether comfortable but he will not be dislodged from it. Colville, on the other hand, is everywhere and nowhere. We see him poke fun at Good-man, but we also hear him plead the Good-man's cause with directness and passion and with no hint of burlesque. He is, we judge, either on the fence, or has so lately entered the blessed pasture of the Anglicans that he has not forgotten what can be said on the other side. He is not sure of himself and hence cannot be sure just what kind of poem he is writing. We need not praise his poem unduly but we can value him as an example of one of the characteristic dilemmas of his time.

Our next satirist, William Cleland, is a man of far greater pith, clarity, and political energy than Colville, and his life like his poems has a certain firm distinction about it. As a Whig, Cleland fought in the battles of Drumclog and Bothwell Bridge. He survived both and escaped to Holland, returning in 1685 to assist in Argyll's unsuccessful campaign. Again he escaped to Holland and returned finally to be shot while defending Dunkeld against a force of Jacobite Highlanders in 1689. He was then, though not yet thirty years old, a Lieutenant Colonel of the Camerons, a regiment composed of Covenanters who had decided to support the cause of William of Orange.

Cleland's collected verse, published posthumously in 1697, contains two long hudibrastic poems notable for vigor, the first of which is *A Mock Poem, upon the Expedition of the Highland-host: Who Came to destroy the Western Shires, in Winter 1678.*

The resistance of the Scotch Covenanters to the settlement of the national church was long; but year after year it was worn down by the threat of poverty and beaten down by armed force, by capital punishment and other punitive measures. The main body of Presbyterians accommodated themselves to the legal church, until the Covenanting nucleus seems to have been largely made up of sects like the Cameronians, who denied every sort of political allegiance. Of these, Burnet affirms with what may appear to be unnecessary intellectual caution that "this is undeniable, that men who die maintaining any opinion, shew that they are firmly persuaded about it,"[1] a generalization that is sufficiently safe.

One of the greatest offenses of the religious rebels was their persistent frequenting of field meetings, or conventicles. In 1670 the Conventicle Act was passed in restraint of this custom, but enforcement proved difficult, as is evidenced by subsequent measures. Persons who did not inform the authorities about conventicles that came to their knowledge were liable to fine, imprisonment, or banishment. As high as 2,000 marks was offered for the apprehension of leading preachers. At last landowners, large and small, were required to offer guarantees that their tenants would not frequent conventicles. But in 1677 the owners informed the authorities, quite sensibly as it seems, that they were not able to prevent the field meetings. Thereupon Lauderdale ordered some of the Highland clans, together with a body of the regular army and militia, to be quartered on the recalcitrants in the southwest. The Highlanders remained some five weeks among the nonresisting population and caused great privation and misery. This visitation was called the invasion of the Highland Host.

In considering Cleland's poem, it is necessary to remember that the Highlanders had never felt the beneficent warmth of the Presbyterian faith and furthermore as they differed from the Lowlanders in faith they differed just as strongly in manners and customs. Hence they were hated as irreligious and feared as barbarous. The faith of Hudibras was no more abhorrent to Butler on philosophical grounds than was the appearance of the Highlanders to Cleland.

The action of the poem is confined to two scenes. In the first "the Squire" addresses the Host to explain why they have been called together and why neither Lauderdale nor Archbishop Sharp has come to speak to them. In the

[1] G. Burnet, ii, 308.

second scene an emissary from the oppressed counties con-
fronts the members of the Scottish Council to protest
against the presence of the Host and to ask for relief. He
is told that there is no relief unless the Presbyterians obey
the law. These two speeches and the direct burlesque
description of the Host comprise most of the poem.

The most interesting thing about the faults of the
Presbyterians as presented by the Squire is that they are
all overt actions and actions against the state. It is not a
matter of what is right, but of what is legal. And herein
the satirist seems particularly well justified in his presentation on account of the air of legalism that seems to thicken
around all questions of religious policy during the period.
No party is free from it. Even the Cameronians, in eschew-
ing all political allegiances and responsibilities, character-
istically expressed their views in proclamations and mani-
festoes. It was long after the Stuart period before all
political disabilities were removed from nonconformists;
but at the time of Cleland's poem religious nonconformity
was still too likely to be construed as active sedition.
Hence the Squire has practically nothing to say in his
speech about what Presbyterians *believe*. He, and the
government, are concerned over what they *do* in the form
of holding "hill-side fleetings, Rebellious and seditious
meetings." There they "rail the Clergie and the State,"
condemn noblemen for immorality, speak evil of the king's
person, accuse the bishops of being too close to Rome, and
even allege that the duke is controlled by his wife. They
write and read seditious books and pamphlets. They come
to their meetings armed, while even the women carry
clubs. Hence the loyal clergy are terrified. Nevertheless,
the chief aim of the duke in trying to suppress the meetings
is not to purify religion but to preserve the king's prerogative. He suffers too much from the gout to come to speak

to them, whereas the archbishop is too busy with deciding weighty questions of the Church, such as

> If Presbyterians, or Witches,
> Deserves in Law the Sharpest touches.

The Highlanders need have no doubt of the strength of their orders, however, nor need they fear punishment for any outrages they may commit.

The complaint lodged with the Council against the invaders carries the poem somewhat out of the region of burlesque, because it is for the most part a direct, passionate and, with one exception, a historically just appeal for protection. The exception is that although the speaker accuses the Host of murder, authorities appear to agree that actually no Covenanters were killed during the invasion. The complaint on the spoiling of the country and its inhabitants seems, however, to be more than justified by the undisputed facts. The Highlanders, says the speaker, even though they stole nothing, would still destroy the land through the daily charge of one shilling sixpence per man, and the consuming of such vast quantities of victuals that but sixty occupy quarters that should be sufficient for sevenscore. The despairing temper of the Covenanters and the inflexibility of the administration are pointed in four lines:

> If ye have no reliefe to send us,
> Goe to, dispatch, eat up and end us.
> They answer'd if yea'll not conforme,
> Yee must resolve to byde the storme.

The sober intensity of these lines makes it the more remarkable that through most of the work the poet was able to touch with a light and scornful hand a subject which evidently moved him deeply. His description of the Highlanders themselves is excellent,

> Some might have judg'd they were the creatures
> Call'd Selfies, whose customes and features,
> Paracelsus doth discry
> In his Occult Philosophy.

They can move about in bad weather because they cover themselves with tar, or at least they are as black as though they had tarred themselves. The common sort are bare-headed, barenecked, and bare from the navel down, to the distress and ruin of decent women. Long dirks dangle between their legs. The leaders wear blue bonnets, plaids, brogues, and slashed coats, and carry shields and two-handed swords—so much furniture that they indeed have "need of bulk and bones." The pictorial impression left by the poem—and it does leave a very strong one—is that of a race of bloodthirsty giants come down from the mountains to devour the simple folk in the valley, and it is this strong impression of fantasy which keeps the poem above the level of a declamatory tract.

This element, also, together with the form of the verse, links the poem to *Hudibras*. More important, however, is the consideration that however obstructive the Covenanters appeared to the Episcopalians, they were in their own eyes the patriotic and legal inheritors and defenders of a national church on their own model. And it is well to bear in mind that, scarcely a dozen years after the Host harried the southwestern shires in the interests of Episcopacy, the government by bishops in Scotland received its final blow under William's settlement, and that although the Covenants were not renewed, Presbyterian and not Episcopal forms were recognized as the only ones at once national and legal. It may, therefore, not be running too close to paradox to say that from a national point of view the bishops were as distasteful to Cleland as the Independents and Presbyterians were to Butler.

The next subject on which Cleland tried his wit was the attitude of the clergy toward the Test Act passed by the Scottish Parliament on August 31, 1681, and the result is a very adroit poem indeed, the *Effigies Clericorum*.

The Test Act was passed under the influence of and in

the presence of the Duke of York. It was designed to insure political obedience and episcopal conformity among all officeholders, civil and ecclesiastical, excepting that the family of the duke was not to suffer political disability on account of religion. In brief terms, the Test required subscription to the Scottish Confession of 1592, and the admission of the king's supremacy in all civil and ecclesiastical matters. Those who subscribed to it affirmed that they were under no obligation to the Covenants, that they would never deny the royal authority, that they would attempt no change in church and state as then established, and that they would never assemble in any meeting to discuss political or religious matters without permission from the Crown. The Act as passed was contradictory; in fact it is said that the article requiring subscription to the Knoxian Confession was inserted in the hope that the Parliament would not pass an act which in one clause asserted Christ as the head of the Church and in the others placed the headship in the king. But it appeared, alas, that no member was familiar with the old Confession, except Sir James Dalrymple who proposed the amendment, so that the whole Act was passed with its whole weight of indefinability upon it.

Since our author had no immediate personal connection with the clergy's uncertainty over the Test, he is able to deal with the subject with a certain irony and suavity lacking in the former poem. It doubtless did his heart good to see Episcopal and indulged Presbyterian ministers alike faced by a Test which required them to submit themselves entirely to the king and ultimately to a Catholic king; he is amused at the prospect of describing "How some refused, and yet conform'd." He cannot call on the Muses to aid him in his task; he must rely upon local inspirations with the hope that they will hold good, even though all the fairies left Scotland when Knox came—an unusual attitude for a Covenanting poet. He says

For I am verie apt to think
There's als much Vertue Sonce and Pith
In Annan, or the Water of Nith,
Which quietly slips by Dumfries,
Als any Water in all Greece.
For there and several other places
About mill dams and green brae faces,
Both Elrich, Elfs and Brownies stayed,
And Green gown'd Farries danc'd and played:
When old John Knox, and other some
Began to plott the Baggs of Rome
They suddenly took to their heels,
And did no more frequent these fields.

Such a passage suggests that though Cleland was a Presbyterian he owned a spiritual resilience not common to all his contemporaries in that faith.

The author does not trouble to give any very positive clues to the identity of the speakers in the poem except that of the Cavalier, the "Courtlie Clergie Man" who presides. He seems intended, on account of his insistence on the wishes of the administration, to represent Alexander Burnet, who succeeded to the primacy after the murder of Archbishop Sharp in 1679. Burnet appears to have been an extraordinarily nervous and fearful man, depending greatly on the support of the civil power for order in the church. On account of the apparent lack of personal satire in the *Effigies*, therefore, it will perhaps be best to state and contrast the various clerical attitudes toward the Test which the poem enlarges upon. The entire company seems to be governed by the assumption that no matter what is said, the Test will finally have to be taken. An air of helplessness and desperation hangs over the meeting.

On the lowest level there are those who knew that they must take the Test to sustain life. This point of view is best expressed by "A pluffie cheek'd red Bearded Mannie" who fears that they will lose their professional reputation through having talked against the Test in any respect; he hasn't been so frightened in twenty years. Before he will sacrifice his manse and glebe he will ponder the Test fully, for "When Men can get no Right, They're forced to use some bitts of flight." This position must have been held by many men in the face of successive oaths required in Scotland, as indeed it is likely to be held in any society in which the authorities attempt to gain a feeling of general security through subscription to formulas. We shall return to this position later in summing up the poem, for cynical as it is, it constitutes the final strength of the government in this question and must have colored decisions of the clergy that were arrived at from other grounds.

The next important attitude with regard to the Test is that it is not inconsistent with itself nor with the beliefs of those present at the meeting. This view is presented at large by "Sophee." He says that to declare Christ as the head of the church is to put in a safeguard against Rome, while to affirm the supremacy of the king is to protect the nation from "Precisness and Lanaticisms." Christ and Charles II are "coordinate" heads of the Establishment. His hearers must distinguish

> A head that is Coordinate,
> From that which is Subordinat,
> A head in sensu Proprio,
> From one in sens Analago
> Distinguish me a head Per se
> From per sequellam, flowering frae
> The power (of) Christian Magistrats;
> Which with the same coagulats.

Such a passage strikes the modern reader as excellent fooling, and no doubt the satirist relished it as well. But it suggests quite clearly the difficulty in which generations of Erastian apologists found themselves.

Sophee receives a pat answer from the point of view of the rulers themselves—"Who," he is asked, "ever yet did plead, To be an Analogick Head" of anything? Sophee had better keep his logic out of affairs and save it to deal with

> Chimeras, Atomes and void places,
> And for imaginary spaces
> For Occult Qualities and Unions,
> Instincts and Summulists Opinions,
> (To tell your young Logicians,
> What Father Aristotle means.)

A third very important attitude toward the Act is that it represents pure "Hobbism" and that if it is subscribed to there are no defenses left against popery. The churchmen have, it is true, been at fault in submitting to one after another of the wishes of Charles II; but they did so with the tacit understanding, as they thought, that no such drastic limitation on the government of the church by the church as the Test represents would ever be placed before them for their agreement.

In short, the loyal churchmen are driven into almost the same position which the Covenanters had always held. They are shown in this poem as objecting to a state domination which had at all times been implicit. Now that that domination is explicit in the present and promises to place them in future in submission to a Catholic sovereign, they do not know where to turn. But however they squirm, it is clear to the Cavalier, apparently, what most of them will do.

> You're at the present hote and wanton:
> An empty Pantrie, and toom Pots,
> Will make you look like half-drown'd Toats.
> Look on good Fellows and advise it,
> Warr's sweet to them who never tryes it.

The *Effigies* is a distinguished satire because it brings into focus all the major problems of theory and practice that had troubled Scotland for years and would continue to do so for years to come. The irony of the poem is that the

Episcopal party is caught and embarrassed by the state, the very power to which it was accustomed to turn for support. A Presbyterian satirist in taking advantage of the moment, produced a burlesque which is a worthy imitation of *Hudibras*, especially in its airy handling of abstractions, and which is by implication a clever vindication of the position taken by moderate Presbyterians.

Since Cleland was personally involved in the issues concerning which he writes, it would have been strange indeed if he had treated his subjects with absolutely consistent raillery throughout. His lyric and patriotic passages and his dramatic passion are necessary results of the conditions under which he wrote. It may be that the poet took a certain wry satisfaction in embedding his personal feelings in the lighter masonry of burlesque, and realized a sardonic pleasure in using Butlerian measures to ridicule Anglican policy. Cleland, it is evident, was not an extreme Cameronian, for the extremists of this sect, like the Fifth-Monarchy men, acknowledged political allegiance only to the kingdom of God, whereas our satirist came to be content with the kingdom of William. Nevertheless, he is, so far as I know, the only Presbyterian who tried to turn the tables on Anglican and Tory by using hudibrastic satire. While not outside of the literary tradition, he, like Trumbull in America, is outside of the political tradition in this form.

Both literary and political traditions join in the work of Archibald Pitcairne, who wrote *Babell*, a hudibrastic poem dealing with the Scottish General Assembly of 1692. This work remained in manuscript until 1830, when it was published by the Maitland Club. Pitcairne was a famous doctor of medicine, possibly an atheist or an agnostic, probably a deist, and certainly a Jacobite. He was near enough to the issues of contemporary politics to be malicious, remote enough from them to be playful, and one of the most sophisticated intelligences to use burlesque verse. This quality is the one which places *Babell* most surely in the tradition of *Hudibras*. In order to understand the bearing of the poem, it is necessary to glance at the status of the Kirk in the years just preceding that meeting of the Assembly which Pitcairne burlesques.

The first parliament to meet in Scotland after James came to the throne confirmed and continued the provisions of the Test Act, the prohibition of conventicles, and the treasonableness of subscribing to either the National Covenant or the Solemn League and Covenant. When, however, James proceeded in 1686 to proclaim free worship for Catholics, he also dispensed to Presbyterians of the less fanatical sort the right to hear their own preachers in private houses, later extending the privilege so that those of every faith might meet anywhere, except in the open air, provided that no seditious utterances were made at the meetings. With the exception of the Cameronians, the Presbyterians, little as they approved of state interferences and permissions in theory, availed themselves of their new freedom. Their fear and distrust of Catholic toleration were, nevertheless, great, and the abdication of James was the occasion of rioting in Edinburgh and the riotous ejection of episcopal clergymen from parishes in the south and southwestern parts of the country. The extreme Cameronians, in particular, seem to have looked upon this political overturn as a godsend to religion and were the most violent party in turning incumbents out of their houses as well as their churches. The moderate Presbyterians in January, 1689, addressed William in order to defend their having taken advantage of James's indulgence and to appeal for his favor in establishing Presbyterian forms as the only legal forms throughout the country. In April of the same year, as part of the Claim of Right, the hierarchy was abolished, the abolition being confirmed by

Parliament in July. It is somewhat curious that this act as finally passed did not mention Presbyterianism specifically, but provided that the king should establish in Scotland such religious forms as were preferred by the majority of the people. Presbyterianism became, however, the national form in spite of the large Episcopal sentiment in the northern counties, and the General Assembly convened in 1690, for the first time since 1653. For the present purpose it is sufficient to note that no mention of the Covenants was made in this meeting, and that although three Cameronian preachers were admitted on their own petition, the Assembly made no move to include more of the "left-wing" Presbyterians nor to work toward union with any of the Episcopal party.

Quite naturally, however, King William wished to have as large and as well unified a communion as possible in Scotland. Accordingly, before the next meeting of the Assembly in 1692 he took measures toward a union of the Episcopal clergy and the Kirk. He proposed to the former that they should submit to Presbyterian government, and subscribe to the "Confession of Faith, and the Shorter and Larger Catechisms, now confirmed by act of Parliament"[2] in matters of doctrine. This formula the clergy accepted and sent a delegation to the Assembly. But the Assembly was not warm toward accepting the overtures, since, if they had been accepted, the Presbyterian members would have been outnumbered. The address of the clergy was "killed in committee," and the king's commissioner dissolved the Assembly. The meeting did not disband, however, before the moderator had insisted

that the officebearers in the House of God have a spiritual intrinsic power from Jesus Christ, the only Head of the Church, to meet in assemblies about the affairs thereof, the necessity of the same being first represented to the magistrate.[3]

[2] Quoted in Grub, III, 329.
[3] Quoted in Grub, III, 330.

The members of the meeting, after they had decided for themselves to reconvene in August of the next year, went their several ways. This ignoring of the desires of William by the Presbyterians almost as soon as they had regained power through his support supplies the subject matter of *Babell*.

The moderator of the Assembly addresses the meeting as the cream, or rather the scum, of the Kirk, and sets the tone of the proceedings by declaring that no one should be so foolish as to think that the Presbyterians will practice the idle virtue of forgiveness toward the Episcopal clergy. The evils perpetrated by the curates for the last twenty-nine years are in fact unforgivable. Neither should it be supposed that the followers of bishops will ever forgive the Kirk for its previous resistance to authority. The curates have been the cause of many ills; their actions by no means create the presumption that they would make loyal members of the Kirk; they are lax in discipline; they have swallowed everything inimical to Presbytery— the Act of Supremacy, the Declaration, the Test Act; they are Arminians, Cassandrians, Socinians, and are in general "Too favourable for all Kings." What is perhaps worst of all, they believe that men enjoy free will to do good; that men are damned not by God, but by their own errors; Sunday is not a fast, but a feast; and they are accustomed to read heathen languages instead of Presbyterian divines, to preach morality only in their sermons, and to maintain salvation may be found in obeying the precepts of the Gospel, "which is contrarie to sence."

The moderator is seconded by "a skabbie fellow" who declares, after carefully turning his back on the king's commissioner to show that he is present against the will of the Assembly, that the two churches can no more join than Presbyterians can prosper under a king, or that a man can be at once a king and a Presbyterian. The first day's meeting is broken up by a peaceable member, a "Laodicean" who pleads for love and charity on the authority of St. Paul. He is shouted down as a madman, a papist, another "Dr. Oates." His proposal creates great disorder that is subdued only by a great voice that bellows "Let's pray to drown the noise." When the Assembly comes together the next day the thought of peacemaking still rankles, so that another member who pleads for amity narrowly escapes a beating.

As might be expected, Pitcairne is not entirely just in his picture of what took place at the Assembly. For example, he makes the moderator object to Episcopal coöperation because that clergy will not subscribe to the Covenant, whereas the Covenant was not then an issue. In the same way the moderator's closing speech on the headship of the church is burlesqued into the statement that

> In all Humilitie,
> We'le with his Majesty comply
> In anything that we think fitt;
> Beyond that we'le not stir a bit, . . .
> Our right is founded on the Word,
> And we'le maintaine it by the sword.

The poem as a whole is, nevertheless, both powerful and adroit. It depends for its effectiveness principally on the burlesque presentation of abstract ideas; on the other hand, the comparatively brief descriptive passages are done in sharp and felicitous phrases. Perhaps the best passage of this sort shows the members of the Assembly in various ridiculous postures,

> Yet all these postures did agree
> Exactly in deformitie.

The poem is more highly polished than the others mentioned in this chapter and it emphasizes the recurrent fear of the opponents of Dissent that the craft, and the ignorance, the obstinacy and the democratic tendency of the unorthodox prove in the long run harmful to state and church.

Indeed, when another quarter century had gone by, it appears that the vitality of the Kirk and the significance of poems burlesquing it had considerably diminished. William Meston, in writing his chief poem, *The Knight of the Kirk*, was handling a theme long turned stale, and had little more than a sort of lazy facility with which to freshen it through his verse.

Meston was born in about the year of the Revolution and died in the year of the last Scottish insurrection, 1745. The record of his life is meagre and melancholy. He is reported to have been a good classical scholar, philosopher, mathematician, and wit. But he was an unsuccessful schoolmaster, and his patrons, the Keiths, being supporters of the Old Pretender, he was on the wrong side politically, and he seems to have existed somewhat precariously.

Oeconomy was none of his talent; for he entertained a most perfect contempt for money. His friend, his bottle, and his book, were his sole enjoyments.[4]

Meston's more important poems were published separately and anonymously between 1720 and 1738; his works were collected and published in Edinburgh in 1767 in what claims to be the sixth edition, but what appears to be the first. The works, minus the Latin verse, were republished in Aberdeen in 1802.

According to the anonymous editor, "Satire was his natural weapon, which was very poignant, and in which he studied chiefly to imitate Butler."[5] Almost all Meston's poems are, indeed, written in the measure of *Hudibras*, but of these we have occasion to mention only three.

The most considerable poem, and the best known, is

[4] Meston, *Collected Works*, p. vii.
[5] *Ibid.*, p. xii.

The Knight of the Kirk: or, the Ecclesiastical Adventures of Sir John Presbyter (1723). Meston seems to have had in mind an extensive burlesque on the entire course of the Reformation, in which Sir John's career was to be traced from Rome to Geneva and thence to England. Only the first canto was published, perhaps because of the poet's vicissitudes and dissipations, but more likely because he found that the subject was really exhausted by his first attempt. The belaboring of Jack Presbyter was almost if not quite played out as a literary game.

Sir John was brought up to manhood by those three nurses of the Reformation, "Sedition, Pride, Hypocrisie." Once grown, he is unable to live at peace with anyone, especially with monarchs, and therefore he furnishes himself with special armor. He has no helmet, but his head is so well "fortified in every part, I mean by nature, not by art," that he need fear no harm in that part of his anatomy. He wears a brass mask through the crevices of which he can see "scandals, plots and fornication," and "the proper minute to rebel." He carries the league and covenant in his hat in place of a feather, and a pair of gauntlets equally adapted to thumping men or pulpits; his body is protected by a half doublet that is "cudgel, sword, and reason proof." His hobnailed shoes are made to tread "on crown'd and mitr'd heads." As for the rest of his character and abilities, he lacks justice and mercy, but he is adroit in furthering his own interests; he owns no real learning, but he knows his own jargon and all languages, except English and Latin; he believes that swearing, except for gain, is evil, but relies on lying because "It is the life of the old cause."

The Knight's charlatanism, like that of Hudibras, is interesting. He is deep in alchemy, Rosicrucianism, palmistry, and fairy lore, but he is low in mathematics, since to understand a true science entails too much intellectual effort. He knows that the earth is flat. But he is naturally an authority on division of all kinds and especially on the divisibility of matter. He has found that a "louse's lug" can be cut in such thin slices as to cover Great Britain, Ireland, Hanover, the Spanish dominions, the Indies, Poland, Muscovy, Russia, Flanders, Germany, and Prussia and that a louse's tooth can be made into so large a number of coffers as would contain a supply of gold 20,000 times as great as England's treasure. He has developed also many mechanical devices. He can inoculate Tory children with Whig blood; he has an air pump to clean his conscience of former obligations, a microscope "to see the smallest cracks of Monarchy," a balance "For weighing conscience with gold," a weatherglass to gauge the public credit, a scale to measure the plots in men's heads, and a Procrustean bed to which he fits all his adherents. At a comic auction he offers among other articles

> a Hook will stipends fisup;
> And here is Ars'nic for a Bishop.
> Here is a spade and other tools,
> For planting colleges and schools,
> And rooting out the bishop-weed,
> And sowing covenanted seed.

On the whole, the direct description of Sir John is too close an imitation of Butler to be consistently convincing. Meston quotes from Pitcairne as well as from Butler, paraphrases passages from the latter, and sometimes practices what looks like inexact quotation as when he writes "In perverse stiff antipathies," in place of Butler's "In odd perverse antipathies."

When the satirist actually invents his action, however, and gives up the effort to produce a Scotch twin for Hudibras, he achieves something in his own right.

The last incident of the poem is a debate between Sir John and a lay elder over whether lay elders and deacons should be deprived of voting in the session and whether the minister should have absolute veto power over the acts of the session. The arguments are lively and the lay elder whose trade was

> Schismatic soal and upper leather,
> With lingel to unite together,

is an effective burlesque figure. By far the best part of the action of the poem, however, is that which includes Sir John's encounter with a highwayman. This incident is prefaced by a burlesque argument on the theory of Hobbes concerning the state of nature and the contractual source of sovereignty.

Men in the state of nature, so the argument runs, "Exactly of the self-same size" were unruly as the seed of Cadmus, and weary of fighting among themselves, chose "a Rector, A hoggan-moggan Lord Protector," to rule them. Thus they gave up their power to

> The King, who still is answerable,
> To th' origin of power, the Rabble.

Once Sir John has stated his political theory, he is required to make it good by surrendering his purse to M'Gregor, the highwayman. The latter admits that their ancestors may have divided the world between them, but he is sure that his never intended him to be in want. In want, however, he is; his natural right to wealth has been violated and Sir John must help him to regain his rights. M'Gregor scorns the Knight's appeal to the protection of the law.

> Tush! quoth Mac-Gregor, Never flinch
> From principles, nor spurn, nor winch:
> Ne'er talk of laws 'gainst nature's right;
> You know far better things, good Knight:
> These cobwebs you have all swept down
> By sweeping off your Sov'reign's crown.

As for his purse:

> Produce it, Sir, or you shall know,
> I'll make a state of nature's blow,
> As cleanly cut off all your treasure,
> As you cut off the head of Casear.

The Knight then turns to the proposition that the purse is providentially his own, using as analogy the argument advanced to Queen Elizabeth by John Knox that she reigned neither by hereditary right nor by the consent of the governed, but by providential right. Nevertheless, M'Gregor snatched the purse on the providential maxim "Major vis est majus jus." This incident is freshly conceived and vigorously written in the true spirit of *Hudibras*.

The second poem by Meston that requires notice is *The Man and His Mare. A True English Tale.* This appears as one of *Old Mother Grim's Tales* which were originally brought out in London in 1737. Six of the tales are written in hudibrastic meter, but only the *Man and His Mare* has a definite satiric point; it is a satire on English foreign policy from the accession of William to that of George II.

A man has a mare which turns vicious from too good living and runs away. She is found by a wandering trooper who rides her into Flanders "to find the glory which he had lost the year before." The soldier wins nothing but a broken neck and the mare passes into the possession of a lady, apparently the daughter of the soldier. Only she or her brother may ride. The next owner is

> a hum drum clown,
> Adorn'd with Capricornus' crown,
> And with a Scaramouch's phiz.

He is "Mynheer Corniger" to whom the soldier had formerly bequeathed the mare. But the new owner rides so awkwardly that a servant must lead the mare for him. He has a son, indeed,

> A strange fantastick Gillipagous
> Begot by Seignior Priapus,

but since he is heir apparent, Mynheer takes care that he shall not learn to ride. Instead, he leaves the mare to grooms and lets her out for hire. Sometimes when he rides her himself he asks an honest man to acknowledge that he is the true owner. If the man refuses, his throat is cut and his money taken. The mare carries great burdens, takes troops abroad and carries dung for the owner's farm.

There is a neighboring gentleman who holds his rich property peaceably and furnishes a great deal of corn and hay for the mare. Corniger nevertheless trespasses on his estate and knocks him down, though neither Corniger nor the mare is the gainer. Some day this blow will be repaid.

Corniger begins to give himself airs and is full of hypocrisy and impudence. He tries to feed the mare on South Sea weed and nearly kills her with it. Finally he dies. Gillipagous, his son, after trying to ride the mare and failing, gives her to Jockey Bob, a fellow who has been brought up by the gypsies to cant and lie. He overworks the mare and starves her almost to death. The poem ends:

> I wish the Man his Mare again,
> My tale is done, say you, Amen.

Mob contra Mob: or, the Rabblers Rabbled, is the account of an attack on the kirk of Deer by a mob of Tories and malignants, even a few Catholics, as well as Presbyterians. The attack fails and one of the Presbyterians proposes a parley to prove to the defenders that the attackers *ought* to win. He is opposed and overcome by a plowman whose final speech contains the real significance of the poem. He points out the end of Presbyterianism as a powerful and coherent political force:

> Sir, what you call the good Old Cause,
> Appears so full of Cracks and Flaws,
> Nor Art nor Skill the same can solder,
> It grows the crazier the older,
> And now is put to a hard shift,
> When Tories come to lend a lift,
> And Kirk-dragoons are rais'd to back
> The Gospel-work you undertake;
> Besides the Revolution Foot
> By standing long hath got the Gout.

In fact, Presbyterianism by losing much of its ancient intractability no longer offered a rich field for the satirist, and satires on the unorthodox needed new objects if the old ideas were to be used with effect. This is not to suggest, however, that the spirit of burlesque in Butler's manner died with William Meston.

V

HUDIBRASTICS ON THE METHODISTS,
THE IRISH, AND THE DUTCH

THE LINE of Dissent in England remained practically un-
broken, for nearly as soon as the Presbyterian question
was worn out, the Methodist question arose. Only sixteen
years separate Meston's *Knight* from the first hudibrastic
attack on Whitefield. Nothing distinguishes the attacks on
the Methodists from those made on previous sects except
defective wit; the substance is, with but one exception, the
same. Ignorance, lust, hypocrisy, and pride mark the new
sect as they marked the men who were responsible for the
death of Charles I. The only new defect is that of humani-
tarianism.

Whitefield is the first Methodist leader burlesqued in
hudibrastic verse, in a poem published shortly after his
return from Georgia, and called *The Methodists*. The anonymous author starts in a tone of rational restraint which is
drowned in vituperation long before he is ready to stop.
All men, he says, hope for salvation, but differ infinitely
in the means of attaining it. Rome kept the western world
subject until its power was checked by the jealousy of
kings. Thereafter, mild toleration became the rule in
England, Elizabeth being particularly "lenitive and mild"
in matters of religion. This beneficent condition was
spoiled by the "lazy" reign of James, which "Nurs'd
various Sects." In spite of the trouble these have caused,
Rome had been held in check in England until the Civil
Wars. Then her machinations endangered the moderate
Church of England by way of "Light-horse Presbyters,"
Baxter, Calamy, and the Quakers. These diverse people

have all been inspired by Lucifer, who very likely has brought forth his "new religious Brood," made up of "all the various Sects in One." This latest society, instead of trying to separate from the Establishment, tries to stay within it, the more to undermine its power, and to prepare for the ultimate triumph of Lucifer and of Rome. Whitefield will be the latest saint in the calendar; he will

> Hasten on impending Fate,
> Big with another Forty-Eight.

As we read passages such as these, we can be thankful that Butler did not pretend to be a political prophet, and that he was content to leave fantasy in his poetry instead of obtruding it on history; for Whitefield is not a political figure. The dominant tone of *TheMethodists* is not fantasy, or burlesque, or wit, or humor; it is fear. Fear, not fantasy, is the note struck again and again until it gives a cracked and tinny sound in poet after poet who tried the measure of *Hudibras* without realizing the courageous stoicism of its author.

No previous hudibrastic poem, so far as I know, ridiculed Dissent for humanitarian leanings, or for upsetting the relations of master and servant—two charges that occupy an important place at the close of the poem. The fact that these criticisms appear shows that the strength of Dissent had become increasingly nonpolitical, and that religious lines were being drawn less and less according to differences in creed, and more and more according to the social interests of the communicants. Whereas Butler burlesqued the desire for power hiding under the disguise of religion, our present author burlesques the Methodists' desire for money masked as love of the orphan. This aberration on the part of the new sectarians ranks with their pretension to humility as exhibited in ostentatious preaching out of doors. In other respects the arguments of the poem are those already familiar in previous works.

The attempts to blend the burlesque with other moods of poetry will be discussed in a later chapter, but we must not leave this poem without remarking its curious blend of the burlesque and the moralistic. The following couplet is very fair burlesque:

> And pack their Faiths as Nests of Boxes,
> Which hold a thousand Orthodoxies.

But is it obviously far away from the tradition suggested by these lines addressed to Whitefield

> The Place that foster'd thee despise,
> And by Enthusiasm rise.

The next three poems against the Methodists are far more consistent in style, but do not merit more than brief mention. *The Progress of Methodism* deals chiefly with the probable profits made by Whitefield and Wesley from the "gainful Trade" of preaching, and the probable carnality of love feasts, and the probable unsoundness of a creed on which the chief exponents cannot agree. "If they no better can agree," so the author concludes, "I'll e'en stick close to where I be." *The Methodist and Mimick*, by "Peter Paragraph," relates how a Methodist tried to convert Samuel Foote and got a tongue-lashing in return. Ignorance and a tendency to rebellion are again the chief points of attack.

> Cromwell like you did first pretend,
> Religion was his only End;
> But soon the Mask away did fling
> Pull'd down the Church, and kill'd the King.

The Methodist is half sententious on the theme of how all good things suffer corruption, and half vituperative on the satanic qualities of Wesley, particularly his stirring up of the lower classes. The author finally commends his enemies to God, who

> tho' his goodness you resist,
> Can even spare a Methodist.

The works just mentioned are important only in showing the persistence of the idea that Dissent is esentially dishonest and politically subversive. The Methodist theme was, however, the occasion for one of the most readable and impressive of all hudibrastic poems, called *Hudibras in Ireland*. The date of publication is uncertain, but is probably between 1825, a year referred to in the text, and 1828, when the restrictions on Irish Catholics began to be removed. The author remains anonymous, but he is obvously a Catholic, and almost certainly an Irishman.

In his poem, he pretends to give an account in six long cantos of the progress of two Methodist missionaries sent from London through Cork, Clonmel, Waterford and "a village on the Suir." Hudibras, the leader, is an Englishman; his squire, George, a Scot. Whether such a pilgrimage was actually made I have not been able to determine; it is certain, however, that the personal peculiarities of the main actors in the story are subordinated to the shortcomings of their belief as seen by a Catholic.

The author is most explicit in comparing his design with that of Butler. The Methodists, he says, are so much like the Puritans under Charles I "that their history would seem incomplete were not the achievements of some modern Hudibras chanted by some one of the satirical attendants at Parnassus." The Methodists seem not so violent as the Puritans, but they are nevertheless just as dangerous as the Puritans to the peace of families and of the state. Hence the author hopes that he can render as great a service as Butler by preserving "a portion of the rising generation from the contagion of Revivals and Bibleomania." He will proceed carefully and document his satire.

Butler's chief object was to exhibit in the strongest light the defective logic and the suspicious virtue of the enlightened and the elect of his time, similar is the intention of the present composition, the most inclusive reasoning, the most contradictory opinions, attributed to the Gospel-mongers, may be traced back to some weekly, monthly, or quarterly report of their own.

The modern Hudibras who is the hero of the present story is a lineal descendant of the original character. Although the latter failed to win the hand of the widow, as Butler relates, he was successful in wooing "a serious Christian maid" later on. A son, the second Hudibras, was born to this couple, a precocious lad who had arrived at the knowledge and manners of a minister at the age of four. The strain was too great for his character and he grew up to be part saint and part scamp. He in turn begot a son, Tertius Hudibras, who in the present story is the chief apostle of the Methodists for saving the Irish from the bondage of the pope.

This young man is physically attractive, especially to women, a great Bible-reader, something of a dandy, full of cant phrases, and essentially ignorant. He and his Scotch squire, "Geordie," are chosen at a dinner in London, and they set out with courage after having swallowed a rich meal and good draughts of port.

The first day of the meeting held at Cork is a success since no Catholic thinks the remarks of the missionaries important enough to warrant a reply, but opposition develops on the second day. Here the author really takes hold of his subject. It is a "bonny sight" he says, to see how Anglicans and sectaries, Moravians, Methodists, Swedenborgians, Brownists, Quakers, and Free Thinkers are all so deeply worried over the condition of the Irish, and how fervently they hope

> T'soothe our feelings by deriding,
> Together bind us by dividing.

As a matter of fact he cannot see that the Bible-reading nations are morally or intellectually superior to the supposedly priest-ridden Irish. One has only to look at their newspapers to see that they enjoy

five times more crim. con. business, robberies, breaches of promise, deliberate and unprovoked murders, false swearing, bastard-making, and suicides, than in the most benighted regions of Popery.

England, particularly, is as hypocritical as she is ostensibly devoted to the cause of Bible-reading. There is no appropriateness in her worrying over the souls of the Irish as long as she continues to oppress the people. Her missionaries should

> Go back and tear the penal code,
> Ope t' our commerce its boundless road;
> And when our pangs have been relieved,
> Your word perhaps may be believ'd:
> But while your right shall grasp the brand
> Of persecution, your left hand
> In vain lifts up the holy page.

Hudibras can find nothing but abuse with which to reply. Just as the meeting closes, he is reminded that not only has enthusiasm for the Bible failed to reform England, but that it has even brought on the evils of civil war, and the biblical lawlessness of Cromwell.

The "Evangelical Mussulmans," Hudibras and George, pass on to Clonmel, not yet discouraged by the debate at Cork, and after surviving some stone-throwing, open a meeting. The vulgar are kept out by an admission fee. The argument of this assembly concerns the spiritual authority of the several churches, and especially the authority of the King James version of the Bible. Father Brian'em, a priest, represents that there were plenty of wise Christians before the beginning of the English Reformation, to say nothing of the Wesleyan reformation, and defies the missionaries to enunciate a faith as clear and as secure as that of the Roman Church.

The mission proceeds to Waterford to attack the "Romanish Beast," but is there assured that since no such animal ever existed excepting in the fallible minds of men, no victory over it is possible. They are now afraid to return to London with nothing to show for their labors, and dressed in extra-fine clothes they go into the country to attempt the conversion of the poor clergy. They find a priest who is poor, but learned enough to confuse their arguments. Most of their objections to Rome, he says, are hackneyed and not worth answering. As for their horror at the use of statues and symbols, they should, if sincere,

> Go break the mace in the House of Lords,
> And bare its sinful figured boards:
> Smash the cross upon the crown,
> And pull the nation's standard down.

After another unsuccessful attempt on a Catholic schoolmaster, the two heroes become involved in a burlesque device which is used as a means to bring their journey to a close. Hudibras resolves to marry an Irish girl with many humble relations, who will follow her example and attend the Protestant Church, thus comfortably augmenting the number of saved souls. He finds that the lady he chooses is willing to marry him, provided that he turns Catholic and resigns to her the education of their children during their minority. The Knight reluctantly agrees, depending on changing his wife's opinion after marriage. The Dissenters and the Catholics in turn get wind of his trickery and this final plan of converting the Irish falls to the ground.

From the foregoing sketch it is easy to see that this poem is directed as much at the English policy toward Ireland as it is against the Methodists. The religious part of the argument is handled in a spirit of condescension and of good-natured fooling, whereas the suppression of Irish interests by England occasions stinging and indignant satire. The poem is complicated not only by the diverse objects of its satire, but by the author's feeling of political inferiority and religious superiority. He dismisses the claims of the Methodists with amused contempt, but contemplates the vested interest of the English with fierceness and futility, as though he sensed that the words of a burlesque poem were no more than bird shot when fired against so solid a wall.

Before doubling on our historical tracks to look at other burlesques about Ireland, we may summarize the present section by saying that in general the Methodists took the place of the Presbyterians as the object of hudibrastic satire. While they were not looked on as an actual political menace, they were attacked as disturbers of the peace and scorned as ignorant, hypocritical, and sensual offshoots of the underprivileged classes. In *The Modern Hudibras*, it is true, Methodism has come of age, and commands the interest and the income of the well-to-do middle class, but to the eyes of the satirist, the ignorance, the hypocrisy, and the sensuality remain and have been joined with the economic and anti-Irish interest of England.

The two other hudibrastic poems on Ireland which we will mention are taken up almost entirely with rural pictures, although the first carries the same strain of political indignation and hopelessness that we hear in *The Modern Hudibras*.

It is indeed somewhat surprising, when one is considering any post-Elizabethan historical period, to find that there is still an Irish question, and as time and affairs go on the surprise increases. For with each new campaign, massacre, or famine, one is led to exclaim that surely after this is over, there will be no more Irish. And then it appears that after all the race has survived deportation, war, starvation, and pestilence by virtue, among other things, of a rapid birth rate and the demand for cheap labor on the land, and that at almost any period there is a cottier left to take his part in a travelogue, or an economic report, or a political complaint, or a burlesque poem.

The Irish Hudibras falls under the subject of this book because, although it is a travesty of the Aeneid, Book 6, the title of it indicates a debt to Butler, and because it is a brisk satire, part anti-Stuart and part anti-Irish.

The tone taken toward the Irish, a mixture of ridicule and sympathy, is somewhat hard to explain. The author, James Farewell, who as far as I know owes his modest place in history only to the production of this work, if he was not an Irishman himself, had at least by his own account spent some time in the Pale. He says in his preface that he began to write the poem while he was there, and that his project was "Encourag'd on by the best sort of Gentlemen-Natives of the place, . . . at whose Houses the Author was often entertain'd, to find out their Language, Sports, and Customs." Very likely this association with the Irish, and probably Catholic, gentry lends the poem a certain amenity that would have been lacking had the author been a predatory bigot as well as a foreigner.

The argument of the poem is stated as follows:

The story is that of Aeneas his going down into Purgatory, to see his Father; where you have a Description of the several Limbos there, the Friends and Acquaintance he met with in his Passage; his Complements, and learned Discourses with his Father, Palinure, Paris, and Dido his old Paragon; How, while he was Consulting the Oracle, Macshane, his Piper was kill'd: Where you have a Description of an Irish Cabbin, Cry, Wake, Burial &c. The Ancient Nobility, Hero's and Warriors. The Succession of the Kings, even to the Late Abdication, and the Present Accession of his Majesty, King William the Third, to the Imperial Crown of these Kingdoms.

Within this framework appear pictures of the Irish poor and their method of living: an Irish kern in the character of Charon whose "Glibbs [hair] hung down like Tails of Rats, His Goggles [eyes] flam'd like Eyes of Cats"; an Irish woman "bare-legg'd, bare footed, and bare-thigh'd," splashing with mud above her knees, carrying her stockings around her neck, her brogues on her head to save expense, and bearing her child on her back, throwing her sagging breasts behind her shoulders to give him suck; and the doorless, windowless, chimneyless wattled hut, with straw roof over the sods that served for fire and furniture.

Against a social background such as these pictures suggest, the complaints of the hero, Nees, have the more force and meaning.

Before Nees descends to purgatory he offers a prayer in the Abbey of St. Patrick and vows that if his prayer is answered he will dedicate an abbey and ordain free liquor and tobacco forever. He prays that the land be no longer mortgaged to French and Dutch, that he be allowed to enjoy his few acres, his buttermilk and potatoes, without danger of reprisal, and that his own person may be safe "without Exile or Transplantation." Through the mouth of Shela, the nun who escorts him, his prayer is answered at once by the Devil, who promises

> Thou wilt (but wish thou'dst never) come
> To thy own Country, House, and Home.

Before this end is achieved, however, the streams of Tiffy, Brackney, and Shannon will run blood; he will be disarmed and reduced to beggary by Dutch and English; and although his miseries are chiefly owing to foreign priests, he himself must expect to be blamed for them. He may expect some success against the "Whigs in Londonderry," but his chief aid in war will come from France. The French forces will bring with them an "Abdicated King" who "Three Kingdoms quit, to set up Mass," and who will "Ireland Intail to France." Faced with such a prospect, Nees is content to be taken to hell, since earth seems to hold little hope for him. He was bled of his property under Charles II; under James II he will suffer by the use of the king's dispensing power supplanting the gospel and the law, and under the new rule of toleration "all may have their Liberty To go to Hell."

Although it is clear by the author's admiration for William where his chief sympathies lie, it does not seem that the political bearings of the burlesque are altogether clear and consistent. The hero, Nees, is a Catholic, and it is not likely that he suffered more under James than he did under Charles; nor is it clear how he will prosper under the reign of William. Leaving aside such considerations, however, the total impression that Nees is doomed to ill fortune under any administration, remains. This humanitarian accent is surprising in a burlesque, especially in one written at that time; it is tempered, however, by the author's social condescension toward Nees and by several severe remarks about him such as

> That he has hardly left a Groat,
> To pay for cutting English-Throat.

Some of the themes of *The Irish Hudibras* reappear in *Hesperineso-graphia*, which was published in Dublin in 1724. According to a clipping tipped into a copy in the British Museum, the author is reputed to be "an old Pedagogue, named Moffatt, residing in Killala," and Bond attributes the authorship to William Moffatt or to one Walter Jones. Whatever his name, it seems certain that he was a Protestant and an anti-Jacobite, that he had read *Hudibras*, and that he despised Irish Catholics, or at least poor ones.

The weight of the poem as political satire is not great, since it consists in having healths drunk to "Father James" and the Duke of Berwick and in ridiculing one of the characters for having fled at the battle of Aghrim. The other objects of satire are the superstition and the debased morals of priests and people and the idiosyncrasies of Gillo, the hero.

The story is, briefly, as follows: Gillo gives a feast to a great company and dispels his sadness by a great deal of eating and drinking. The guests having finished the meal, promptly disgorge it to make room for more beer. At this point a fight starts between Bruno, the coward who boasts his prowess at Aghrim, and Redmundo, who challenges the truth of the story. Redmundo is restrained from stabbing his opponent, but finally attacks and routs him. Bruno, however, calls to his friends for help and the fight becomes general. Neither Gillo, by wielding a churnstaff, nor the priest, by preaching, can stop it. The former has his beard set on fire by a candle, while the latter, after receiving a "Vizard of Cow-dung," goes home to his mistress. Bruno meanwhile has hidden under a pile of fodder to think how he can repay Redmundo. He is inspired. He seizes a black cowhide that hangs on the wall, dons it, blackens his face and hands, and mounting a cow backwards, rides among the guests grunting, bellowing, and waving a firebrand. The priest is recalled to exorcise this evil spirit, which he promises to do if he is paid in advance. Bruno in turn promises to retire if he is paid for his tiresome journey from hell. Next, he looses all the cows, finds Redmundo, beats him with a dung fork, and his revenge accomplished, hides before he is discovered. Gillo, finding his cows loose, beats one on the head with an ax. She races about madly. He aims another blow. The ax head flies off and hits Bruno. He starts up and the people, terrified at the apparition, fall into ditches and lie there till morning. Then they declare to Gillo that his house is polluted, but Bruno explains his trick, and peace is restored.

The strength of the poem obviously lies in action of no very refined sort. The most extensive satiric burlesque touches the person of the hero and it is in this part that the connection of the poem with *Hudibras* is clearest. For though he owned the native attributes of being a great card player and a fighter at fairs, he was also a great disputant and logician, not to be confuted, and a defender of paradoxes.

> To show his Skill he'd undertake
> To prove a Goose to be a Drake;

> And often smartly argu'd, that
> An Owl was but a flying Cat;
>
> . . .
>
> All schools of note he did frequent,
> Only for sake of Argument.

Lines like these indicate that though his manners came largely from Ireland, his literary genealogy sprang from the other side of the Irish Channel.

To the burlesque pictures which we have seen of the Scotch and Irish, we will add the portrait of the Dutch afforded by *Hogan-Moganides*.

Burlesque is a convenient medium through which to express scorn for the object of it; the method loses its clarity and edge when the object for some reason forces itself into the respect of the satirist. Probably some such mixed attitude was in the mind of the author of this poem. For, although he sets out to make the Dutch ridiculous, he rather succeeds in expressing his jealous admiration of those very qualities which he attributes to them.

He is at any rate clear about his inspiration for the poem. To one "M. L. Esquire" who has presented him with a copy of *Hudibras* he addresses a letter, printed at the close of the volume, in which he protests that his own work conforms "to your Commands, not to the Pattern you gave me . . . Unimitable Hudibras, who as he had the honor to be the first, so must he survive the Ne plus ultra of all Burlesque." This might perhaps be taken as mere modesty on the author's part, but once it is admitted that *Hogan-Moganides* runs into difficulties which *Hudibras* escapes, it seems clear that those difficulties rest in the scheme of the poem and not in the shortcomings of the author as a writer of burlesque verse. As a matter of fact, he is an excellent writer. His charge against the Dutch, however, is that they have grown rich by skill in the manual arts, by adroit diplomacy and by attention to fisheries, foreign trade, religious toleration and hard work in every field they entered. With such a list of practical virtues to work on, most of which he probably admired himself, the author is somewhat put to it to maintain the required critical and superior attitude. It may, indeed, not be going too far afield to suggest that it was impossible for an Englishman in 1674 to write about the Dutch from the same point of view from which Butler regarded the Dissenters, or Colville the Presbyterians. England, it is true, was at last to gain ascendancy over the Dutch in colonies, trade and diplomacy. But the beginning of the ascendancy was still some years ahead. At the close of the third Dutch War in 1674, the two countries were still competitors. Now drawn together by similarities in religion, now thrown into war over conflicting ambitions of trade and empire, they had neighbored each other in jealousy and emulated each other in expanding activity for more than seventy years. And in spite of differences in temperament, it seems impossible for a writer with even cursory knowledge of the recent history of the two peoples to satirize the Dutch as a nation except for those qualities which he himself valued.

Such considerations, however, do not prevent the author of the present poem from having allowable burlesque sport with the genealogy of Hogan. It has been supposed that he spawned from pork, or butter, or cheese,

> Or like his Damm, from Ocean Froth,
> The antient Liniage of the Geti;
>
> . . .
>
> Or by some Stallion of the Floud
> Begot on Monster of the Wood.

As a matter of fact, his parentage includes all these suppositions. His father was Alman, a ferryman of Delft who invented red herrings; his mother was "Guddy Allgut." Allgut during pregnancy so longs for buttermilk that she drinks the entire supply in the country; she then brings forth Hogan's elder brother,

> A Son of Neptune, and of Mars,
> Full fraught with Engines for the Wars.

Thereupon her thirst returns, and after drinking a vast amount of brandy she gives prodigious birth to Hogan. He after

> Sayling throw borders of Pamphilia,
> By straits of Abdomen and Illia,
>
> . . .
>
> Stearing East and by West of Norward,

finally steps out, already three years of age, "six Brie Gammons" in his right hand, a ton of butter in his left, and a shoal of salmon in his mouth. Allgut and Alman die shortly from delight or indignation.

The two orphans are quite unmanageable. Hogan eats enormously. His elder brother cannot assuage his thirst until his guardians take him to the sea. That is his element, and he sports in it to the delight of Hogan. The gossips decide that each infant is the complement of the other, that between them they will found "A State of Sea, as well as Shore," and that it will be true to say of Hogan,

> In every Boat he had an Oar,
> And had a Boat for every Shore.

At home, also, Hogan shows almost infinite energy and versatility. He drains his land of the ocean. He is truant from school, it is true, but in his truancy he carves his name on every kind of object with his penknife. His hand work shows

> In Diamond, Scallop, Chess, and Net-work;
> On Dishes, Platters, Spoons, and Ladles.
> On Drawers, Cabinets, and Cradles,
> On Stocks of Musquets, Locks, and Flasquets,
> On Boards, and Cup-boards, Kitts, and Baskets.

In drawing, in painting, in the conduct of affairs, in building—particularly in diplomatic constructions—he is infinitely capable. His nationalistic spirit, indeed, is so unflinching that,

Hee'd take no wrong, nor do no Right,
And justify 'em all by Fight.

Thus far it is apparent that to the Rabelaisian description
in the poem are added a clear analysis of the national talents
and some rather pointed and succinct passages on them, of
which the couplet just quoted is not the least admirable
example. The most interesting and original part of the poem
is that which deals with the relationship between trade
and religious toleration.

It seems to be commonly accepted that the peculiar
virtues of Puritanism were a direct impetus to capitalistic
growth, that in England the turning aside of the Dissenters
from the main stream of national life directly furthered the
Industrial Revolution, and that, at the same time and somewhat paradoxically, western society became less religious
and more secular in its distinctive preoccupations. Furthermore, as one religious body succeeded another in dominance, during the process of this long social change, the
charge and countercharge of greed and hypocrisy is brought
against bodies who claim to be actuated by high principle.
Mr. Belloc, for instance, thinks that greed was one of the
greatest forces behind the Reformation, and Butler's
charges of greed and hypocrisy against the rebels are
apposite. And I suppose it may be justly said that Henry
VIII had no violent objection to engrossing and selling the
lands of the Church, and that when the Anglican bishops
sacrificed their fiscal importance after the Restoration by
giving up Convocation they sacrificed some of their
sacerdotal importance as well. In any event, the familiar
satiric charge against political and religious opponents is
that they claim to be men of principle whereas they are
really thoroughgoing materialists who worship only the
god of getting on in the world.

The reader of *Hogan-Moganides* is somewhat surprised to
find that this particular assumption, or accusation, does not

appear in the poem. To the Dutch, so the author says, religion is frankly a trade. They tolerate all sorts for the sake of trade.

> Religions he had every one,
> And had so many he had none;
> He suffer'd all, but none wou'd hold,
> And all his trust was in his Gold.

The Dutch, so the author seems to say, may be double-dealers in diplomacy, but they are by no means hypocrites in religion, for they have none. They are frank materialists.

Hence the poem is a satire on a society in which the leaven of Dissent has worked so long that the categories of religion have no meaning. And whereas it seemed difficult at that time to satirize an English politican without reference to his views on religion, or an English man of religion without reference to his political leanings, this social satire proceeds without linking politics and religion, or trade and religion. The word common to both comparisons cancels out, and politics and trade remain. Materialism, the economic factor, has erased the lines of creed.

VI

HUDIBRAS IN AMERICA

HUDIBRASTIC verse in America takes its chief vitality from the brisk, informal description of the manners of the new country, but it is closely connected in idea and in point of view with the English models. The hudibrastic manner appeared early in colonial history in the poems attributed to Ebenezer Cook: *The Sot-Weed Factor, Sotweed Redivivus*, and *The History of Colonel Nathaniel Bacon's Rebellion in Virginia*. These poems, indeed, are more closely related to the work of Ned Ward than to *Hudibras*, on account of their descriptive detail and a garrulous narrative style. Both of the *sot-weed* poems contain touches of satire on Dissent, as in the figure of the Quaker in *The Sot-Weed Factor*,

> Who neither Swore nor kept his Word,
> But cheated in the fear of God.

The poet is chiefly interested, however, in picturing the drunkenness and knavery of the Marylanders as a whole, and the particular venality of the court at Annapolis. *Sotweed Redivivus* is a competently written pamphlet in verse, by no means wholly burlesque in intention or treatment. It is mainly a debate on the subject of improving the finances of Maryland by diversifying the products of the colony. Not only the stimulation of foreign trade by means of a variety of produce is suggested, but the expedient is recommended of limiting the number of acres which each planter may devote to tobacco.

The poem on Bacon's Rebellion is a rather flat performance, interesting in an account of hudibrastic verse chiefly because Bacon's designs are compared to Crom-

well's and his rebellion with the Civil Wars in England.
Even after Bacon's death

> The Rebels for the good old Cause,
> Persist 'gainst Governour and Laws.

Such phrasing shows a clear connection with previous
burlesque verse and carries on a tradition much more
positively marked in the hudibrastic poems occasioned by
the Revolution.

The first of these, *The Association*, was published in 1774
as a burlesque of the proclamation of the Philadelphia Con-
vention of the same year. It consists of a ballad, a recita-
tive, and a chorus, the last being written in hudibrastic
verse. A couplet from the *Virgil Travestie* appears on the
title-page, so that it might appear more appropriate to
place the author of the pamphlet as an imitator of Cotton.
The political and cultural satire in the poem, however,
and some of the riming make the reference to Butler appropriate.

The burlesque argument is that although the Parliament has been useful to the colonies in driving away their
"heathen Foes," the Association will starve its members
and the Parliament as well, if certain acts are not repealed.
If the colonies are pushed, they will prove stubborn. The
Admiralty laws in restraint of trade with "our good Friends
the Dutch" must go, together with the Quebec Act and the
act abrogating the charter of Massachusetts Bay. The
British should not protest the Boston Tea Party, for the
fault lay with the East India Company in sending the tea
in the first place.

The poem is written in an admirably sustained blend of
burlesque and irony; a good example is the comment on
the citizens of the Massachusetts Bay Colony.

> Nor need they, Aid of British Noddle,
> When they think proper, to new-modell
> Their present Form; they'll do't alone,
> They're Statesmen, every Mother's Son.

In 1775 *The Patriots of North America*, a much more elaborate loyalist poem, was published in New York. In manner it is a curious mixture of scornful burlesque, playfulness, and serious appeal. The colonists, the author says, are misled by Hancock and Adams. For they are not really prepared, either by education or by social background, for self-government. They might be excused for rebellion, indeed, had they not been born late enough to profit by the teachings of Locke. That "Apostle blest! of Toleration" had rescued men from the theories of Hobbes and of Filmer. Divine right in fact and in theory is dead. Locke is called upon to pity the present generation for perverting the sense of what he wrote. For though he did his work while faction, sectarianism, and bribery were notorious, he never was the apostle of civil war. He never tried to call the citizens to arms.

The colonials are much freer than were the citizens of England in Locke's time. Furthermore, they are free and wealthy in comparison with the common people of any other country. The French, in particular, are virtual slaves. Yet they contrive to be happy. What is more, their wise men like Diderot, D'Alembert, Montesquieu and Rousseau, "lov'd to dwell" there; and though they deplored the evils of their society, they preferred these evils to the horrors of civil war. The author hopes that even thus late these historical and philosophical reflections will show the colonials that they are acting like ungrateful children and that they must avert war.

It may be supposed that the author got considerable comfort out of this last argument, if he died before the French Revolution. His attitude toward the threatened revolution in America is a blend. It partakes of the attitude of Rousseauism, of constitutional liberalism, and of the American apologists for African slavery. In his view the ideal condition for the majority of people is a "low, unambitious State" of life. True, they are denied power by the laws of heaven; but since they are not tempted by luxury, their morals are likely to be good; furthermore, they are free since they enjoy the protection of the laws. The author assumes that each social and economic class has its own "Sphere," the members of which leave that class only on pain of making themselves ridiculous. The American revolutionaries, says the author with the inexactness which must be pardoned in a burlesque poet, are "Form'd for the Oar, the Sledge, the Saw," and know nothing about those things which were called mysteries of state in an earlier day. Among their class mere literacy is enough to turn a citizen's head. As a whole, the colonies are like runaway schoolboys from Eton, ignorant both of general history and of their own traditions. They exult in temporary liberty, as long as masters and parents are distant. Then they reflect "How weak their plans, how scant their Purse," and "Car, Vir, Mar, Con, Rhode, Mass, and Ham" sink to quarrels and recriminations which last until they own they have been misled by Hancock and Adams, and "Their just Subordination own" to their lawful master. If they do not do so they will have to conform to the "puritanical Modes . . . Whom God, nor Man, could e'er reform." The author is sure that the supremacy of King and Parliament will be preferable to theocratic domination.

Perhaps the most interesting thing about this poem is the small amount of political argument in it. The weight is placed on social, economic, and philosophical considerations. Social inadequacy and intellectual narrowness here as in *Hudibras* are the chief arguments against attempting political change.

This point of view is found again in *A Continuation of Hudibras*, a poem against the Revolution published in London in 1778. This work seems not to have circulated widely; at least, a manuscript note in the British Museum copy says that the author, Joseph Peart, probably a solicitor, had only enough copies printed for his friends. If this is true, the author seems to have been unduly modest; for while his poem ends in a mist of allegory, most of it is an admirably versified attack on the social and political pretensions of the rebelling colonists and of their sympathizers in London. Quite specifically the American Revolution is traced back to its source in the English Civil Wars; it is hard to say whether political precocity or social presumption is the greater sin in the eyes of the author.

The poem begins in mock-historic vein. Hudibras, when his "cause of Dudgeon, Had scarcely got one foot to budge on," calls a meeting of the defeated Presbyterians. Of course Pryn, Bastwick, and Burton, that much-belabored trinity, were there; but there were other men of low degree present

> Who genealogists suppose,
> Descend from men averse to marry,
>
>   . . .
>
> As Will's son, Harry's son, and John's son;

other colonial names as well shone at the meeting: Adams, Hancock, Otis, Cushing, Deane and Franklin,

> Whose sage descendants we shall see,
> Shine forth in the next century,
> Proving their wishes to inherit
> That discontented factious spirit
> Disguis'd with hypocritic zeal,
> I'th'name of love of a common weal.

Hudibras rises at the meeting and, surveying new realms like Satan, sums up the results of their long struggle against monarchy. He was not aware that King Charles had so many friends left; the Presbyterians have caught a Tartar whom it is not wise to oppose any longer. But there is a new country "rising in the West." Let many members of the party emigrate, there "With natives and with transports mix," beg privileges from the king, and raise a posterity which may in time make the colonies strong enough to throw off their "long dependence." Then, no matter if England spends millions of pounds in defending the colonies against France and Spain, the colonies will refuse to repay one shilling in ten. For, according to the tradition of Dissent, to do so would be "a cruel plan . . . of forcing people to do right." In that new western community tradesmen will become members of Congress, clerks rise to be generals, and paupers will be soldiers, presuming to aim rifles "at men of highest rank." With such a prospect the defeated English rebels should sail West with high hopes, never forgetting their ultimate purpose of overthrowing the English constitution.

The plan of Hudibras is approved. Some members sail, while others stay in England to watch the government and to keep their colonial friends informed. The stay-at-homes finally produce offspring to embarrass the government, such as Mrs. Macaulay; her brother, Alderman Sawbridge; Frederick Bull; John Wilkes; and especially Edmund Burke.

The American descendants get their first chance to hurt the government under George II, when they resist helping to pay for the campaigns against the French. Also it is hard to make men understand the necessities of imperial finance if those men are, like the colonials, both avaricious and penurious. They do not appreciate the true beauties of the national debt, or the ancient glories of Malplaquet, Oudenarde, Blenheim, and Ramillies.

The poem closes with a conventional account of Discord and her machinations and a long and not particularly satirical versification of the Declaration of Independence. The French have inevitably encouraged the colonials to perfidy, but the author hopes that the British arms will be successful and that at last "truth and loyalty shall rise To their hereditary skies." In spite of the rather flat and pious ending, however, we must praise the poem as a whole. It is a clever adaptation of the hudibrastic machinery; but its main interest lies in showing how at least one English citizen evaluated the cause and the motives of the American colonists.

M'Fingal, by John Trumbull, is, of course, the best known American burlesque in the hudibrastic style; more properly, perhaps, the only one that is well known. The author uses the same sort of historical legerdemain that Peart employs in the *Continuation* by relating his hero to the ancient cause of rebellion in Scotland. M'Fingal did not, however, remain true to his original faith; he became perverted to monarchy, and figures in the poem as a Tory.

One of the most interesting things about this work, indeed, is the fact that Trumbull, like the more obscure poet Cleland, was able to adapt a satiric weapon used traditionally as a whip for the middle class to what might be called roughly the popular cause. If the Revolutionary party was not really dominant in 1775, the author is able to give the impression that it was, and to give M'Fingal an appropriate air of stupidity and of social undesirability. If one wishes, he can say that there is a nice literary compensation in the circumstance that more than a century after *Hudibras*, the manner of that poem was adapted to belabor a High-Church monarchist. Or one may say just as truly and perhaps more relevantly that *M'Fingal* is a perfect justification of the fears and scorn expressed by Butler, Ward, and others. For it exhibits Dissent in its own self-contained society, with its own conventions, with the desire and the power to look askance at other forms of religious and political propriety. The wheel turns slowly, but it turns.

Trumbull's literary parentage is not, of course, confined to *Hudibras:* Dryden, Pope, and Gray furnished him models for a number of his poems, and the influence of Gay and

Churchill may be seen in his hudibrastic compositions. *The Progress of Dullness* and the *Advice to Ladies* are far more didactic than burlesque; the fable of *The Owl and the Sparrow* owes more to Gay than to Butler. The two shorter poems, however, no doubt gave the author necessary practice in handling tetrameter and helped to form an instrument which could be used extensively later in *M'Fingal*.

The burlesque of M'Fingal is first-rate political satire. The author uses words with a sense of their actual, concrete meanings; he generally eschews book language except for burlesque effects; and scarcely any of his lines are padded. It is true that the machinery of the vision by which the success of the American cause is foretold is not conducive to interest. Nor does the poet much concern himself with a burlesque of ideas; intellectual playfulness is mostly lacking in the poem. But the burlesque satirist can overcome defects like these if he knows the burlesque connotations of words set in surprising order and if his original concept is one which really lends itself to burlesque action. *M'Fingal* can easily stand all ordinary tests of conception, design, ingenuity and vigor.

Once the Constitution had been adopted, and the political tendencies within the states had begun to solidify into parties, there was great scope for satiric attack and counterattack in verse and prose. Hudibrastics proved serviceable in this war and returned to their traditional uses in the verse of H. H. Brackenridge and of Thomas Green Fessenden.

Brackenridge, like Butler, did not have the temperament to sustain party warfare with any great comfort. Although he was largely anti-Federalist in politics, he supported the new Constitution; and although his sympathies were democratic he never left off satirizing the political pretensions of the relatively uneducated electorate. As an independent spirit he was forced to strike out on one side and then on the other in the difficulties of the Whiskey Rebellion, the constitutional settlement, and the many other problems of frontier Pennsylvania. He maintained an ideal of rationality in times and among people where rationality was frequently something less than a virtue, with the result that he presents a respectable figure to history.

In literature he found his medium in the prose of *Modern Chivalry*, but the hudibrastics of *The Modern Chevalier* which contain the germ of the prose work, are not very readable. The machinery of knight and squire was not only somewhat shopworn by this time; it was out of place. And, as the other poems of Brackenridge show, he was rarely at his ease outside of prose. For point and clarity Fessenden far exceeds him, partly, perhaps, because he discards all traditional machinery except the verse form.

Fessenden launched his chief attacks on the Jeffersonians, but earlier he published a satire on doctors under circumstances which lent an added air of originality to the performance. In 1801 he went to London to attempt to establish an English market for a pump in which a number of business men of Rutland, Vermont, were commercially interested. He arrived at a time when the patent "tractors" of Elisha Perkins were enjoying great popularity and great opposition. These tractors were made of metal in somewhat the shape of an ordinary toy magnet, flat on one face and half-round on the other. They were supposed to carry galvanic virtue and to cure various ailments when the affected areas were stroked with the rounded surface. The inventor and his son who promoted the sale in England must have realized a very considerable profit, since the cost of the contrivance could not have been great and since the tractors sold for five guineas the pair. The popularity of the device failed when an English doctor wrote an article to prove that the effect of the tractors was owing only to the imagination of the patient and that according to his own experiments, wooden tractors served as well if the patient himself believed in their efficacy.

Fessenden's poem, the *Terrible Tractoration*, appears to have been written after the publication of this scientific attack. To some it seems that Fessenden himself believed in the tractors, but I do not find anything in the poem which would make such a conclusion necessary. It seems to me more likely that Fessenden, low in funds on account of the failure of his commercial enterprise, found a good opportunity to exercise his talent for burlesque and to make a little money. The general idea of the poem is that although the silliness of using tractors may be great, the silliness of accredited physicians is even greater. The argument is carried on ironically by Dr. Christopher Caustic, whose practice has been damaged by the "Perkinean Institution."

Caustic, with lancet and microscope and his knowledge of chemistry, was once a great practitioner even to the extent of creating a homunculus very useful to barren noble families. He has plans also for bettering the nature of man which if followed "I dare to venture ye, He'll be an angel in a century," and which place him far ahead of Dr. Price and Godwin. Nevertheless he is "Completely damn'd, the simple fact is, By Perkins's Metallic Practice," even to the point of starvation. He calls on the medical fraternity to attack the force that threatens its scientific supremacy, relying first on words and last on blows to

> Attack Medulla, hight Spinalis
> From where the head to where the tail is.

The poem is short and lively and lacks decisive effect only because it is written in the future tense. There is no actual combat.

The *Tractoration* went through two editions in London in 1803. During 1804, when Fessenden returned to America, the first American edition was published in New York and the author's *Original Poems* were brought out in London. The preface to this volume gives a coherent statement of Fessenden's political temperament and opinions, later given extensive poetical form in his *Democracy Unveiled*.

The author, a thorough anti-Jacobin, considers Great Britain "perhaps the only barrier against an inundation of modern Goths," that is, the French radicals. Hence, he is glad to have his poems published in London, not because they are good in themselves, but because they may inform the English about the "manners, customs, and policy" of the United States, "between whose interests, and those of Great Britain, there subsists a most intimate and reciprocal connexion." He apparently hopes that American Federalists can serve their country by repressing populism, as England serves the world by resisting the French and their ideas. In short, he wishes his own country well, but he mistrusts the future of it. There are too many handicaps to be overcome: republican citizens are notoriously jealous; the voice of the people is by no means true and infallible; too many citizens are "immediately concerned in the affairs of government"; and republican forms have never been tried over so vast a territory.

The *Original Poems* were republished in Philadelphia in 1806, with the original preface and the addition of many other poems on events of the intervening years. The poet's methods, however, do not vary from those which he defines in his *Simeon Spunkey's Political Pepper-Pot*, written in 1798. "The poet," he says, "Over the Union courses rapid And squibs each jacobinick saphead," producing thus "A kind of Hudibrastick summary Of politicks, and other flummery." He persists in detesting the French, but changes his attitude toward England somewhat. She is still our "good mother," but she must restrain her lion in respect to our neutrality, lest Paul Jones "break his bones." He adds that he distrusts "president-palaveration" on the subject of peace being a safe substitute for national preparedness.

Fessenden's most considerable work is found not in the volumes already discussed nor in *Pills, Political, and Philosophical* (1809), but in *Democracy Unveiled*, which went through three editions in 1805. The poem is an attack on Jefferson, Rousseau, and democracy generally; it is divided into six cantos entitled "The Tocsin," "Illuminism," "Mobocracy," "The Jeffersoniad," "The Gibbet of Satire," and "Monition." The titles do not leave much doubt about the tone of the poem. The poet's purpose is to

> unmask the Democrat—
> . . . who by public good, intends
> Whate'er subserves his private ends,
> And bawls for freedom, in his high rant,
> The better to conceal the tyrant.

A charge like this has a familiar ring, not only because political attitudes are in general highly predictable, but because it is similar to those that have appeared before in this history. The democrat, excitable, ignorant but crafty, greedy for power, inimical to stability, is the enemy of vested interests and of centralized control. He is, therefore, to be controlled and discouraged by all available means, literary, political, social. The democrat is particularly dangerous when he has some sort of theory or philosophy behind him to justify his ambitions and desires. He is heartened, or demoralized according to one's point of view by the writings of Paine, Rousseau, and Godwin. He gets notions about the economic and political perfectibility of the common citizen, as well as views about his moral perfectibility. To make matters worse, he tends to make his progress not by the orderly processes of Christian hope, but by the sophistical methods of human reason. This doctrinaire tendency brings about such logical results as those of the French, who think

> To kill one half mankind were best,
> Just to philosophize the rest.

Liberty as understood in France is the same as that practiced in the Whiskey Rebellion in America. The tyranny threatened by an unrestrained democracy is either the tyranny of the ignorant mob, or the tyranny of despots who, like Napoleon, assume a dictatorship in the name of the common good.

Jefferson is not likely to be a restraining influence in the democracy, for he uses unbridled license with his female slaves, and

> Great men can never lack supporters,
> Who manufacture their own voters;
> Besides, 'tis plain as yonder steeple,
> They will be *fathers* to the *people*.

The lesser lights of the party are rude, untutored, grasping, and dishonest. The Democratic party and the theories behind it must be suppressed if the republic is to prosper.

It can readily be seen that Fessenden allies himself with a point of view that is as old as political theory and as new as the latest election. He is, as far as I know, the only American who has written an extensive hudibrastic poem from the Federalist point of view. His expression is effective as long as he deals with the theories of the opposite party, but the poem falls in quality as soon as the author turns to personalities. He then writes not satire, nor burlesque, but innuendo and abuse that are tiresome and beside the point. Nevertheless, his cantos on "Illuminism" and "Mobocracy" are extremely effective performances. It is a pity that Fessenden, as long as he eschewed all direct action and plot in his poems, did not devote himself more consistently to intellectual burlesque; for he associates ideas nimbly, and is tireless in bringing amusing words and phrases into play. He had, also, a nice taste in light familiar verse, as witnessed by the Vermont vision he records in his *Epistle Excusatory:*

In yonder sable swamp of hickory,
I Simon saw the nymph Terpsichore,
On banks of Otter Creek she blew sharp
On whistle now, and now on jewsharp.

On the whole, this author was by no means a great satirist, but he was an extremely good colloquial poet, using the language with freshness, vigor, and respect. And he was one of the last of those who used hudibrastic verse to re-prove the errors of democratic dissent. After him, the in-fluence of *Hudibras* in America seems to dive underground, or to be diffused into so many channels that the taste and color of the original stream can no longer be distinguished.

We may say, in conclusion, that satires definitely hudi-brastic in inspiration appeared at times when the fear of democratic or populistic tendencies was felt by the classes in power. The composition and the name of this minority party differed with the passage of years, but the fears engendered were on the whole the same. The exceptions are Cleland and Trumbull, and these men wrote from the point of view of powers which "of right, ought to be" dominant, Cleland expressing the feeling of a traditional national majority, Trumbull that of a vigorous Colonial minority. It is possible that the complication of parties and interests finally contributed to the exhaustion of the hudibrastic impulse. Certainly the political point of Butler's work was both justified and outdated as the forces which he satirized regained actual political power.

PART THREE

HUDIBRAS AND THE BURLESQUE MOOD

VII

THE BURLESQUE MOOD

THE MOST casual reading of *Hudibras* shows that large parts of it are not political at all, or political only in the very widest sense. These nonpolitical matters in that poem and in later burlesque writing naturally bear a certain relation to English literary development. What this relation is I shall try to show, in so far as I understand it, by discussing the burlesque mood, the variations of it in *Hudibras* and the forms which it assumed thereafter.

Most of the political burlesques in the hudibrastic manner contained, of course, elements not specially political in their reference and meaning; in addition, there were other poems, written chiefly during the eighteenth century, which are closely related to *Hudibras*, but which contain practically no political elements at all. This latter class, while not large, is important in the history of burlesque, and merits discussion here, especially in view of my belief that those poems bearing a predominantly stylistic relation to Butler's work indicate the relation of *Hudibras* to the later development of burlesque writing in England.

This historical bearing cannot, however, be profitably discussed without some general consideration of what the burlesque mood is, what its limits are, and how it is related to other literary atmospheres. I shall try to give some sort of tentative answer to these questions, in spite of the danger of running into an impenetrable thicket of esthetic considerations in the process, beginning only with the idea that burlesque implies some sort of variation or distortion.

When we try to apply this notion to objects of perception, we run into difficulty at once. We may, if we like, speak of natural burlesque or caricatures. A pollard willow may appear to us as the burlesque of a willow tree. A pine bent or twisted out of its usual shape by wind, a horse ill-favored by nature or a hard existence—such appearances are clearly distortions. But we do not truly succeed in attaching the word *burlesque* to them unless we first imagine that the agency causing the unusual figure is an agency of will and personality. If, for example, we suppose that God moves across the earth changing the shape of objects from normal to abnormal, we may suppose also a vein of humor and irony in His mind and a consequent burlesque in the effects of His works. Such suppositions, even though they should be true, are so begirt with improbability that we generally content ourselves with saying, not that a mis-shapen animal or object is burlesqued, but merely that it is deformed. This distinction between the burlesque object and the deformed or misshapen one does not, it is true, enlighten the real nature of trees, or cows or horses, but it may be very useful later on in distinguishing between real burlesque and apparent burlesque.

Deformed objects are in a way closely related to those deviations from the normal that result from faulty technique or poor vision in art. That is to say, there is a large class of *unintentional* burlesques to which belong oddities in art and in manners. Nothing is easier than for a man to burlesque himself in speech, or costume or action, unconsciously and, of course, unwillingly. The unconscious burlesque in the early forms of art is the sort which is the nearest of any of these types to the general subject under discussion.

The awkward drawings of very young children, so familiar to most people, are a good example of this art which is intellectually and technically undeveloped. Suppose that a four-year-old boy has made a few colored lines on paper, and an older person asks him what they are sup-

posed to be. They, the boys says, are a cow. And so they
are a cow—by fiat. The caption may even have been an
afterthought. But the point is that here, the boy, instead of
giving his family something in the way of satire, or burlesque, or caricature, or even deformity, has blundered into
a symbolism that is both private and incommunicable.
Suppose, however, that this young artist goes on making
marks on paper until his once authoritative symbolism
submits more and more to the tyranny of the eye, and his
eye and his hand begin to collaborate on pictures. Then the
artist will begin to draw forms that, while they are increasingly like cows, are notably and amusingly lacking in
certain accustomed parts, proportions, and physical attitudes. They are laughable, but they are not meant to be;
or, if they are meant to be, it is because the artist confesses
that the conventional and representational cow is still
beyond his powers and he will amuse himself with fanciful
approximations. A similar incongruity between intention
and effect is offered by many ancient and medieval drawings
and carvings, except that in them there is more doubt as
to the original intention. Thomas Wright met this doubt
when preparing his *History of Caricature and Burlesque* and
included certain drawings because, although the intention
behind them might be doubtful, the effect was not.

Nevertheless, it is confusing to call any production
actually burlesque unless the design of the artist was to
make it so. That is, the term can be used without extravagance only of art which has passed the stage of mere repre-
sentation and is a self-conscious variation on a theme that,
in turn, is thoroughly intelligible both to the artist and
to his audience. The act of putting the representational, or
realistic, into some sort of relationship with the burlesque,
as I have just done, brings with it a problem that is peren-
nially interesting in any consideration of burlesque.

The problem arises on account of the theory that few

artistic distortions can be more satirical or more amusing than those natural distortions of action and manners that I have already mentioned, and that consequently the height of burlesque can be reached through faithfully reporting people as they appear. Related to this theory is the one examined by M. Brunetière in *La Maladie du burlesque*, according to which the burlesque mood is realistic and primitive, bringing with it into literature elements of raw reality and vigor which are foreign to the politer forms of expression. Now, it is fairly easy to show, as M. Brunetière demonstrates so convincingly, that there is nothing primitive in the conception or execution of burlesque art. Self-consciousness and sophistication are inherent in it. Self-conscious reporting of actual forms and persons is, however, another matter, and although that is not the kind of burlesque represented by *Hudibras*, it seems to me to have exerted a great influence on later literary manners.

This naturalistic theory provides for the production of burlesque by reproducing abnormalities from real life, but not for imaginative portraits, nor for the distortion of literary manners and ideas such as the parody and the travesty, nor for the touches of fantasy and humor which have a part in the burlesque mood. In France, however, writes M. Brunetière, the imitation of nature was, after Boccaccio, associated with gross and unlovely details. Accordingly, when it was seen that burlesque employed such details, it was assumed to be a naturalistic revolt against preciosity.

En France . . . on a volontiers confondu "l'imitation de la nature" avec la grossièreté pure et simple, ou du moins avec la vulgarité . . . De ce que la grossièreté des termes, involontaire ou voulue, et la bassesse ou la trivialité des sentiments, tantôt rèelle et tantôt affectée, sont des éléments nécessaires ou constitutifs du burlesque, on en a donc conclu que le burlesque c'était le "naturalisme" et par conséquent le contraire du précieux.

On the contrary,

le burlesque et le précieux, par des moyens analogues et contraires, se proposent uniquement le même but, qui est . . . la surprise ou l'étonnement du lecteur . . . Toute autre considération,—didactique ou morale, scientifique ou objective,—leur est entièrement étrangère.

And again, speaking of the same two styles, he says:

Également éloignés de vouloir imiter la nature, ils s'accordent en ce point que le triomphe de l'art est de la dénaturer.

What does this "denaturing" of art, common to the burlesque and the precious, imply in the criticism of English literature? It would seem, first, to mean that either manner, when pushed to extremes, is a good deal like the other in effect—that Euphuism, Marinism, Gongorism, metaphysicism, tend to become something like Butlerism or Priorism. And it means that, in either manner, there is such a mixture of temper and accent that one cannot be quite sure what is in earnest and what in jest. Let it be granted that biographical criticism is indispensable and that it can do much. But, when it has done all it can, how are we to feel about the caprices of Donne, or those of the Cavalier poets, or those of Crashaw, or about the extravagances of the heroic drama? We shall feel, it seems to me, that there are a great many beauties of form and language, but that we are not so sure about the meaning of the men behind them. We come to sense a narrowness of scope—a tradition of language and of literature more than a tradition of living.

Do we sense anything different when we turn to English burlesque and travesty in the Restoration? In particular, do we gain a different impression from *Hudibras?* The answer is not positive on either side. In the light of M. Brunetière's remarks it seems, however, that *Hudibras* is stylistically not so isolated a phenomenon as has sometimes been supposed. I doubt whether Butler could have written, for example, *The Lady's Answer to the Knight*, if he had not been fairly adept in the mode of expression which he puts into the Lady's mouth. And, the meter aside for the present, I should challenge anyone to identify the following lines as burlesque, and as Butler's burlesque. In their pretty sententiousness they might have been lifted from a second-rate dramatic lyric of the court, or from a first-rate heroic drama:

> But Love, that its Extraction owns
> From solid Gold, and precious Stones;
> Must, like its shining Parents prove
> As solid, and as Glorious Love,
> Hence 'tis, you have no way t'express
> Our Charmes and Graces, but by these:
> For, what are Lips, and Eyes, and Teeth,
> Which Beauty invades, and conquers with?
> But Rubies, Pearls and Diamonds;
> With which a Philter Love commands?

Courtly verse? Yes. Burlesque? Certainly. And I believe that this passage could be matched in its essentials, by anyone who enjoys the game, from the works of a dozen seventeenth-century poets who are not now considered to be writers of burlesque. And how they considered themselves at any given artistic moment, who can say? The important point here is that as Butler did not invent his verse form, neither did he invent the kind of mental and literary ingenuity with which he filled it.

Enough has been said about naturalistic and realistic burlesque, perhaps, to show one of the fruitful methods of describing not only *Hudibras* and the imitators of it, but an even wider class of burlesque productions. At any rate, these notions will be tested by applying them to Butler's poem.

First of all, what are the characters and the action of *Hudibras*, and what are they like? It is a pity that, as far as I know, no imaginative illustration, that would really interpret them to us, has been made. Hogarth's illus-

trations are drawn in a stolid spirit that, in comparison
with what Butler says about his characters, is both confusing and dull. Hogarth draws matter-of-fact pictures of
certain types of English life on the lower levels of a half-
century before with almost exactly the same feeling with
which he makes his moralistic pictures of contemporary
types. The character sketches and scenes of action in the
poem, on the other hand, are certainly not moralistic, nor
matter-of-fact, whatever else they may be. Neither are they
realistic. When one thinks of the descriptions of the Knight,
of Ralpho, and of the rabble, it may seem for a moment
that their figures have been fully and carefully presented.
How could it be otherwise, with all the words which Butler
lavishes on them? But when one returns to those actual
words it is clear that no such meticulous presentation of
character was made nor, probably, intended. The sense of
ordinary personality in these people was our own illusion,
or perhaps, no more than a conventional assumption.
Witness the famous beard of Hudibras. The author faithfully tells us that it was shaped like a tile, and that it was
tawny in color, a mixture of whey, orange, and grey. This
much is said, and said well, in six lines; and it gives us all
of the actual beard that we shall see. But these details do
not give us our impression of the beard, or at least they do
not give the impression of that decoration which is gained
at the end of the forty lines that are devoted to the beard.
This detail of the hero's appearance comes into the reader's
life as a man's beard, as a beard on a man—an eccentric
beard, but indubitably a beard. But the beard does not remain mere beard. It becomes a prophetic, a symbolic, an
apocalyptic, a monstrous beard, to

> Tell with Hieroglyphick Spade,
> Its own grave and the State's were made.

If we try to look at or to imagine the other characters, we
get but little help from the author. Ralpho, he says, is a

tailor, but he wastes no words on his looks. Crowdero has an ear "warped"—warped probably by crowding his fiddle under it—a grizzled beard, and a wooden leg. Orsin is only "grave." Bruin has fur, of course, and a ring in his nose. Talgol "shone with oil." Magnano and Colon have no physical features. Trulla is "stout and tall." We get no clear picture of Whachum, nor of Sidrophel, nor of the Lady. The characters, in short, are shadow pictures, for all that the author tells us to the contrary, and could not be delineated in any other medium unless the artist drew deeply on his own fancy. In the passages of action, therefore, the characters move and fight as shadow pictures and not as men and women. But, one may say, what of the actual slapstick comedy in the poem, like the attack of Whachum and Sidrophel upon Hudibras:

> But Hudibras was well prepar'd
> And stoutly stood upon his guard.
> He put by Sidrophello's thrust,
> And in, right manfully, he rusht,
> The weapon from his gripe he wrung,
> And laid him on the earth along.
> Whachum his seacole-prong threw by,
> And basely turn'd his back to fly.
> But Hudibras gave him a twitch
> As quick as lightning in the breech.
> Just in the place, where Honor's lodg'd,
> As wise Philosophers have judg'd;
> Because a kick in that part more
> Hurts honor, than deep wounds before.

The action, while it lasts, is swift, no doubt; but all that it tells us about the characters is that they have the form and the parts of men; and it turns out besides that the interest of the action is not in the action itself but in the last four lines of comment on it.

To bring evidence to show that *Hudibras* is not a realistic poem may seem to some to be a wasted effort. It is a necessary one, nevertheless, partly because of the kind of inference drawn from Butler's work by later writers, and partly because one cannot get a right notion of *Hudibras* itself without accepting the labor of fancy and imagination which Butler imposes on his readers. The vagueness and generality with which he treats his characters are indeed essential to the tone of the poem as it was actually written. One may test this statement by supposing that we could prove the identity of all the actual persons to whom Butler alludes, that we had portraits of them and knew their intimate biographies. Would that knowledge change our reading of *Hudibras* essentially? Probably not. To put the matter in another way, when one reads the active parts of Butler's burlesque, he is somewhat in the position of a producer of a play who has been handed little more than the speeches of his characters with voluminous notes on them—notes that tell something of what the actors shall do, but that chiefly digress on what odd and foolish notions they possess, and that give little hint of how that oddity and that foolishness are actually to be bodied forth in physical burlesque. The reader is, in short, handed an intellectual fairy story with some dramatic elements in it, to be illustrated from his own imagination. Particularity and verisimilitude about persons are essential to eighteenth-century burlesque, but are no part of Butler's business.

When we have dismissed the possibility of realistic burlesque in *Hudibras*, we have left a succession of speeches by the characters, with the author's comments. A list of the types of people and of occupations that are treated in a burlesque way would exhaust the list of stock subjects of satire, and the very fact that there are so many subjects adds importance to the way in which they are treated—to that question of burlesque style that has always fascinated the readers and the critics of *Hudibras*.

In thinking about Butler's style it is helpful, first of all, to distinguish between the "burlesque" form of verse

used for direct satire and the same verse form used for indirect satire or burlesque. As a matter of practice the contemporaries and followers of Butler used the term *burlesque*
for any verse of hudibrastic form and general tone, without
paying much regard to the nature of the fable itself. To me,
however, the direct quality of Part III, Canto II, is considerably different from that of any other major division
of the poem. The persons and events that it attacks are
more definite, and it carries a cargo of moral indignation
along its forensic stream from which the other cantos are
largely free.

> And now the Saints began their Reign,
> For which th' had yearn'd so long in vain,
> And felt such Bowel-Hankerings,
> To see an Empire all of Kings,
> Deliver'd from the Aegyptian Awe
> Of Justice, Government, and Law.

One may think that the eloquence of this passage differs
little from that of the following, from Part II, Canto II, in
which Hudibras describes the Independents in the person
of Ralpho:

> An upstart Sect'ry and a Mungrel,
> Such as breed out of peccant humors
> Of our own Church, like Wens, and Tumors
> And like a Maggot in a Sore,
> Would that which gave it life, devour.

The great difference lies in the context. For in the first instance the reader is led to recall specific history, whereas in
the second, he is encouraged to further enjoyment of the
interplay between two fictional characters. Again, in the
first passage, it is Butler's indignation that is expressed in
a tone which shows that the objects of satire were in his
opinion not only intellectually confused but morally cul-
pable. In the second passage, on the other hand, the indignation of Hudibras is broken and, so to speak, intercepted
by burlesque rivalry between him and his squire, and we

think how foolish both of the actors are. In other words, while Butler uses the same medium throughout his poem, the burlesque verse is most properly burlesque when he is dealing with fanciful material. It is in such places that his witty garrulity has the sharpest and most distinctive point. There the satire is indirect and is subordinated to the artistic design of elaborating eloquently on the wrong-headedness of the characters. Butler uses subtle intelligence to show the subtle unintelligence of his chief male characters. And here is what seems to me the mainspring of his burlesque method—the use of elaborate literary devices to give in minute detail the lapses and endless deviations of the human intelligence. Lack of good sense, not lack of good morals, is the main occasion of his burlesque.

At the same time, the polished rhetoric of *Hudibras* has a literary reference as well as a social one. Butler's humorous allusions to the heroic manners of romance are well known, and I have mentioned earlier his lack of regard for the contemporary heroic drama. More definitely, there appears to be a fairly clear relation between *Hudibras* and Book II of *The Faerie Queene*, which concerns the adventures of Sir Guyon, or Temperance.

Spenser introduces Sir Huddibras, the companion of Sans-loy, as

> an hardy man;
> Yet not so good of deedes, as great of name,
> Which he by many rash adventures wan,
> Since errant armes to sew he first began;
> More huge in strength, then wise in workes he was,
> And reason with foole-hardize over ran;
> Sterne melancholy did his courage pas,
> And was for terrour more, all armed in shyning bras.

The main outlines of this character are not far from those of Butler's hero, and his association with Sans-loy increases the similarity. The "tawny" beard of Hudibras is matched by the "tawny" beard of Furor, the son of Occasion. It may be that Butler took not only the name and character of Hudibras from Spenser but that he was assisted in filling out the picture by the characteristics of Sans-loy and of Furor, as well as by Braggadochio and Trompart, who are successively presented in opposition to Guyon. There the direct debt to Spenser appears to cease, for Butler was not writing a decorative and moralistic drama. Nevertheless, the parallel between his story and Spenser's is engaging. While Spenser gives imaginative shape to the forces that hinder moral temperance, Butler gives a picture of what people do and say who have no intellectual temperance, and of what their civic actions mean.

In doing so his method is a tacit criticism of Spenser's method and of the romantic method generally, in that he complicates and intensifies the inner nature of his chief characters, whereas in Spenser the complication of temperance with various kinds of intemperance is not intensified within his characters. Again, Butler's descriptive passages in burlesque mood are not far from some of the more emotional passages in Spenser, such as the description of the hag, Occasion, as she urges Furor to do more harm to Phedon:

> And ever as she went, her tongue did walke
> In foule reproch, and termes of vile despight,
> Provoking him by her outrageous talke,
> To heape more vengeance on that wretched wight;
> Sometimes she raught him stones, wherewith to smite,
> Sometimes her staffe, though it her one leg were,
> Withouten which she could not go upright;
> Ne any evill meanes she did forbeare,
> That might him move to wrath, and indignation reare.

I do not mean to imply that this picture is exactly amusing, but the lines about the lady's staff give a touch of the ludicrous to the passage which it survives with difficulty, and which suggests the mood in which some of the ungainly fighting in *Hudibras* is recorded.

Spenser

By making these references to Spenser, I do not intend to say that Butler took the work of his predecessor as his chief literary point of departure. In fact, he often refers to the whole field of romance, notably the French, as the object of his wit; it does seem likely, nevertheless, that Butler took from Spenser some suggestions for his hero, and that as he proceeded to parody romantic conventions, some of them no doubt were referable to Spenser. Of greatest importance, however, is the observation that romantic writing, like "metaphysical" writing, tends toward the burlesque as it becomes more specialized and extravagant. In this regard, it is not misleading to say that Butler achieved effects intentionally that Spenser, and Donne and Cowley achieved unintentionally.

What then are the kinds of writing in *Hudibras* that are definite enough to have given suggestions to later burlesque writers? First comes the description of characters distorted in appearance and action—figures that are clearly not meant to be copies from life. Second comes the studied extravagance of word and phrase that is partly, I judge, the effect of the author's own subtle intelligence, and partly a conscious parody of heroic and courtly verse. The travesty of romantic conventions is a third element which, though it is not confined in its reference to any one work, does have some definite connection with the Second Book of *The Faerie Queene*.

This element of travesty had something to do, I should say, with limiting the literary availability of *Hudibras* to imitators. In the first place, the travesty in *Hudibras* is general, not specific; directed against a habit of mind and of expression, rather than against a single author. Furthermore, the writer of a travesty is far more likely to go directly to the work travestied for his suggestions, than to a former travesty. At any rate, *The Irish Hudibras* is the only hudibrastic poem I have seen to combine any considerable travesty with other burlesque elements and satire.

The elements of *Hudibras* to have a wider effect were the descriptive and active on one side, and the more elegant, abstract, and witty, on the other. No later writer was able to handle both kinds with the success of Butler, but each took from the original example as much as he could use. Without attempting to describe every poem among the imitations, I shall choose those which are most representative of the two chief kinds of hudibrastic writing, taking first those whose chief content is the manipulation of abstract ideas, and whose authors were apparently most interested in the logical and verbal finesse of Butler.

Of those writers whom we have already mentioned, Pitcairne is preëminent for the finesse and delicacy with which his arguments are turned. Cleland at his best is a close second. Pitcairne, however, was temperamentally more remote from his subject than was Cleland. He was also a man of far more intense and active intellect, who, although he did have a sense for effective description, took most pleasure in the manipulation of ideas. D'Urfey, on the other hand, while far more lively than the others, is too deeply pleased with plots and pictures to achieve the intellectual playfulness of Pitcairne.

VIII

INTELLECTUAL BURLESQUE

AFTER 1700 a number of burlesque poems were published which dealt more or less directly with rational divinity, and which have in them a minimum of direct satire or of literary satire. Accordingly they belong among the casuistical children of *Hudibras*.

It is a pity that when John Asgill's *Argument* was burlesqued, the work was not done by a first-rate wit. Asgill, a lawyer and a member at different times of both the Irish and the English Parliaments, was either crooked or muddle-headed, and had the misfortune to end his life in a debtor's prison. As shown by his *Argument*, he had, however, a strong literary gift. As the title suggests, his pamphlet is an entirely legalistic argument to the effect that although God condemned the sons of Adam to death, that condemnation was removed by Jesus, with the result that now God is legally restrained from enforcing his original edict. Hence any mortal who cares to enter a claim to freedom from death can win free translation to immortality without suffering any let or hindrance from death. Asgill's printer set up the pamphlet in short paragraphs of one or two sentences each, like this:

Suppose my Mother died in Childbed, must I therefore do so too? Or that my Father was hang'd, must I therefore be drown'd? Every man possesses as much of Eternal Life as he knows; and he knows as much as he possesseth, and no more.

But in this Composition the Spirit is so perfectly mixed with, and diffused through the whole Body, that we can't now say which is Spirit, nor which is Earth, but the whole is one intire living Creature.

As in leavened Dough, we can't say which is the Leaven, nor which is the Dough.

Clearly this is superior prose, and, just as clearly, it is prose written in a mixed mood, frequently so profound, often so ridiculous, that we cannot tell when we are listening to a profound mystic, when to a pedantic doctor of divinity, and when to a rascal lawyer on a metaphysical holiday. Perhaps the book is its own burlesque and meant to be so; perhaps it burlesques a type of argument in divinity. By Asgill's contemporaries, however, it was taken as serious, and as blasphemous enough to be burned both in Dublin and in London, and to help the author toward the loss of his parliamentary seats.

As far as I am able to find, three burlesques of the pamphlet appeared. One, a clever prose travesty, takes notice of the novel arrangement of Asgill's pages. The other two are in hudibrastics. The lesser of these, *The Death and Burial*, is based on the real or supposed illness of Asgill after he arrived in Dublin. He and his book are very weak; but he need not fear medicines for "They can't destroy, if He can't die." *The Way to Heaven in a String* is a more rugged performance, though it leans rather too heavily on the actual diction of *Hudibras*. In its best passages the poem reaches a blend of informality and point. Asgill, the knight

> never bow'd his stubborn Knee
> In any feats of Chivalry,
>
> . . .
>
> Had no mischance in any Points,
> To dislocate his nimble Joints,
> But such Disasters as befal
> In Battels Metaphysical;
>
> . . .
>
> In sacred scripture he had read
> How Enoch and Elijah fled
> To Heav'n by Faith, and in their flying
> Disdain'd the Common way of Dying,
> Which does Mankind in Thraldom fetter,
> Only because they know no better.

The ingenuity of this poem is the ingenuity of Asgill and its gains its success chiefly because of its fantastic subject. In Asgill's argument we find the same mixture of legalism and mysticism that distinguished the dialogues of Hudibras and Ralpho; but here that mixture is divorced from any political significance. Asgill is satirized mostly as a harmless and amusing eccentric, but partly as a free-thinker who goes too far with his private interpretation of the Bible.

The intellectual vices satirized in *Hudibras* as peculiar to Dissent, appear in a cluster of eighteenth-century bur-lesques as the special mark of secular defections from the Established Church and from officially accepted theology. There are some signs of this point of view in the poem just mentioned, but they are much clearer in *Free-Thinkers*, *War with Priestcraft*, part of the *Four Satires*, and in *Alma*.

These poems vary widely in literary value, but they have a common point of view. That is, all of them criticize more or less good-naturedly the pretensions of rationalism as a medium for discovering ultimate truth. These poets have practically nothing to say against experimental science; as far as one can tell it does not exist for them. What they are interested in is the gradual secularization of the search for the soul and for the truth of God. They fear the disintegration of the church and of morality owing to the growth of the authority of reason. Historically, the process which they deplore is attributed to two main sources; first, to the increased knowledge of Greek and Roman philosophy; and second, to the separatist tendencies made most dramatically apparent by the Civil Wars. The latter have affected the thinking of "Broad" or "Low" Churchmen, which in turn has encouraged deistic or atheistic secular thought. This process has tended to ab-stract the individual from all social institutions—the state, the church, the moral code—and has tended therefore to leave him alone with his own intelligence, an object more absurd, or more dangerous depending on the temperament of the observer.

The Free-Thinkers, occasioned by Shaftesbury's *Letter concerning Enthusiasm*, and according to the foreword written "immediately upon the coming out of that Pamphlet," attempts to show that freethinking is only another name for transgressing the moral code. The free thinker is a free lance in society. Sensual pleasure is one of his chief aims, but, what is more important, he is noted for "Scorning all ties, Divine or Civil." His individualism is centered on preserving and aggrandizing himself; he admits no ties, owns no tradition. He has dropped below the level of the narrow party man in politics, and uses party only for his own purposes. He

> of Lycurgus talks, and Solon,
> And is old Dog, at Hobbs and Toland;
> Knows all Republican Defences,
> And Raves on Cato Uticensis,
> With t'other of that Name, and Brutus
> He daily labours to confute us;
> When Adam dug, and Eve set Onions,
> He says that all Men were Companions;
> That Kings were made but for the People,
> As for the Church was made the Steeple.

From this passage it is clear that in the author's mind the freethinker tended to support antimonarchic causes even though he owned no set policy of his own.

When we turn back from this poem to the *Letter concerning Enthusiasm* itself, we are puzzled to find the points of reference. The difficulty lies in a mental characteristic of this burlesque writer—one which is by no means foreign to others we have mentioned. The others say in effect that the statements ridiculed cannot be true, for if they were true, they would be harmful to society. In any event, the portion of the *Letter* which seems to have aroused our satirist is that in which Shaftesbury argues that the legal restraint of enthusiasm whether noble or ignoble is unwise policy, and that such restraint can lead only to secret growth of the evil it was supposed to cure. Perhaps, indeed, our poet was irritated by the delightful passage in which Shaftesbury imagines the results of a legal restraint on poetic enthusiasm: "we might perhaps see a new Arcadia arising out of this heavy persecution: old people and young would be seized with a versifying spirit: we should have field-conventicles of lovers and poets."

While the brightest lustre of the *Free-Thinkers* is borrowed from its object, the appealing consistency of *War with Priestcraft* is the special property of its anonymous author. Excepting *Alma*, I do not know any other eighteenth-century burlesque that establishes and maintains from a sincerely critical point of view a tone of mockery, light but precise, sharp but playful. This poem omits the pietistic, the oratorical, the patriotic; yet it is obviously written by a religious and eloquent Englishman.

The method is ironic throughout. According to the heading of Canto I, indeed, and the running heads, the name of the poem is *The Fall of Priestcraft*. The preface extols the great and ancient names of free thought, those eminent for worldliness, ambition, and self-interest: Alexander, Philip, Caesar Borgia, Pope Alexander, Julius Caesar in secular affairs; Mahomet, Arius, Athanasius, the Quakers and Muggletonians in religion. Fortunately, the law and the army are two professions free from the taint of freethinking, for in one the freethinker is reprimanded, in the other, court-martialed. In modern England, however, he is free to carry on his work in the church and in the community at large.

According to the title-page, the *War* is "Dedicated to the Celebrated Author of Christianity as Old as the Creation," the book by Matthew Tindal which had been published two years previously, in 1730. Tindal and Anthony Collins get more attention in the book than any other modern authors, though Toland and Woolston, among others, are alluded to. Passing by the usual charges of sensuality and self-seeking, we find that in the eyes of the satirist the freethinkers, like the old Independents, represent anarchic and divisive tendencies.

Freethinkers, so the argument runs, are Knights-Errant, in the Cause of Truth; they fight the rest of mankind with intellectual weapons for mankind's own good.

> So, near a Century agone,
> The Parliament of—Forty One
> Rais'd for their King a mighty Force,
> Who fought against him Foot and Horse,
> Until most loyally they took
> Their Prince,—and brought him to the Block.

The poem will trace free thought

> From Epicurus, down to Tindal
> Our future Canto's shall relate,
> That Tale, which shall thro' Ages pass
> Of Knight 'yclept Sir Hudibrass.
> At least if we should rise no higher
> Than pari libra—with Matt. Prior[1],
> We still shall Comfort have o' this,
> Our Verse and Subject's of a Piece;
> And we with reason may expect
> The Poem may outlast the Sect.*

Free thought, whether coming from India, Egypt, Greece or Rome, whether descended from Eve or from Lucifer, has made greatest progress in modern England through Lucretius—in Creech's translation;

[1] Author's note on this passage: *"This is not designed as any Reflection on Mr. Prior; his Alma is without question a very entertaining Piece, but his Poetry is not altogether so regular as Butler's, he has sometimes suffer'd three Lines to rhime, and has even made use of Alternate Rhime, neither of which agree by any means with Hudibrastick Verse."

> his Labours teach
> (Translated by the Hand of Creech)
> Our Pupils—Priestcraft to defy
> With tuneful Infidelity;
> Tho' had he still remained in Latin
> Not one in ten—had e'er got at him.

The members of this new sect ought to have some common mark which would distinguish them from the rest of the world, but a creed is difficult, even one made up of negative affirmations, when each member is supposed to be separated from all others. Yet there should be something

> Which may as well Free-thinkers note
> As Quakers are—by Querpo Coat;
> Something in us peculiar too,
> As Circumcision in a Jew;
> A Sign—which may our Sect explain,
> Yet not precise—or full of Pain
> As theirs,—but somewhat degage,
> As a Free-thinker's Faith should be.

Their only real signs are disbelief, a desire to destroy the church, and an obtuse intelligence.

> Each Soldier in himself a Chief,
> All over arm'd with Unbelief,
> Impenetrable Brass they bear
> Unpierc'd by Argument in War.

Their boldness yields only to the terror of death and the frequent impulse to suicide. But they should not take this way out. Why should they not, like the Puritan sects

> in spite of Seas and Shelves,
> Seek Country's wild as they themselves,
> And bless the Winds that brought 'em there,
> Transported safe—from Common—Prayer;
> Might they not make as good an End on 't
> As Quaker,—or as Independent?
> Could they not grub up woody Region
> With the same ease they did Religion,
> Then in their room,—(what most they lack)
> Plant Atheism and Tobac?

The freethinkers are very little worse than the deists

> Who tho' they plainly don't deny
> The Being of a Deity,
> Yet limit, censure, and define,
> Which answers still the same Design,
>
>   . . .
>
> Nor give weak Minds so harsh a Trial
> As from an absolute Denial.
> So when in Year of Forty-One
> The Parliament their Stir begun,
> Tho' refractory all the while,
> They left not off their courtly Stile,
>
>   . . .
>
> Gilding black Deeds with outward Beauty,
> Much Reverence,—and little Duty!

The deist explains that creation is not of God but of nature. What nature is he cannot say except that it provides for the making, breaking, and remaking of forms. Or he, like Charles Blount, imagines

>   a boundless Mind,
> Which animates at once the All,
> And every individual;
>
>   . . .
>
> A Democratic Deity;
> A Light emitting living Beams,
> An Ocean which from Being streams:
> And hence 'tis clearly understood,
> That all which we behold is G–d,
> From Sun and Moon, to Flea and Louse,
> And henceforth equal—Man and Mouse.

With so glorious a faith abroad in the nation, one can look forward to being rid of the parsons and to applying the money given for their support to reducing the national debt.

I have quoted extensively from this work not only because it contains the best hudibrastics of a rather genteel sort after those of Prior, but because by statement and implication the poem draws together several of the orthodox attitudes toward movements dangerous to the health of the church. Again and again, in many if not in most of the poems which we are considering, the deadly parallel is drawn between the course of democracy and the course of dissent in religion and of rationalism in philosophy. The satirists from Butler to Fessenden had a good deal of right on their side. There *was* danger that the more people learned to read, the more the popular and unphilosophical Press would thrive, and vice versa; there *was* danger that the more people went into dissenting communions, the less would they patronize the Establishment; there *was* danger that the more people sought a basis of religion beyond historical Christianity, the less obedient and fervent would be their allegiance to accepted philosophies and rites, and that their religion of whatever name would become more common-sensical and secular. The fallacy and the final weakness of all burlesque attacks on religions and philosophical dissent are found in the mechanical assumptions from which they sprang and in the naïvete of their assumptions concerning the origin and the nature of religious and political allegiances. The burlesque writers assume (whether sincerely or not is generally impossible to say) that a defection from the Establishment is a defection from religion and that political opposition to the *status quo* is a denial of any coherent political allegiance. They do not intimate by accent or intonation that a man is an animal just as religious as he is political, and just as political as he is religious. In their view, religion and politics are, for the Englishman at least, fully developed entities, the inheritance of every citizen, and that rather than being developed from the properties of men's minds, they become in a sense the property of men of mature age. And as property they can be bequeathed or conveyanced in a thoroughly legal and constitutional way. These satirists were, indeed, victimized by the nature of the controversies in which they took part, by the dominant legalism of them and by the corresponding absence of an adequate theory of normal and abnormal psychology. Their effectiveness lies in the clarity with which they saw general social tendencies at work within the institutional fabrics which they were defending.

The author of the *Four Satires* has a word to add on the effects of the new philosophy and expanding journalism.

> Nay, in this Age, Apprentice-youth
> Burn with Enquiry after Truth;
> Can, at one Glance, in Pamphlets see
> That all are made, by Nature, free;
> Tinctur'd with Tenets new, deny
> Or Legal or Religious Tie
>   . . .
> Beat Constable, at Parsons jest,
> And think as freely as the best;
> Swear, whore, drink, reason, and dispute,
> And are—Philosophers minute.

Our main interest in this publication lies, however, in the author's prefatory remarks on hudibrastic verse and on Dryden's criticism of it. Dryden, he says,

was not infallible and we may say of him in regard to Burlesque, what he said of Milton with respect to Rhyme, that he did not make use of it, as having no Turn that Way. . . . Having chosen heroic verse, that was a sufficient Reason for him to declare it to be the most or only proper Measure. As no one in his Time could rival him in that Excellence, he would exclude all other.

Later on, the *Alma* of Prior was to convince readers that the eight-syllable line does not necessarily constrict thought and that it has a force of its own.

The Dignity of Hudibrastic Style, if, by the by, it has any, is so far from being debas'd in his Hand, that it is surprizingly improv'd, nay, perhaps carried to its highest Point of Perfection.

If Prior's example is not stronger than Dryden's precept, still the author of the *Four Satires* must choose hudibrastics as "most natural to the Levity of my Genius."

This reference to Prior suggests what must have been a fairly common attitude toward his work among burlesque writers and suggests also the fulfillment of a tendency which had been at work in burlesque verse ever since the publication of the first part of *Hudibras*. Prior, it seems to me, carried the writing of elegant hudibrastics as far as it could go, but he was following a natural course of development. We have seen that practically as soon as *Hudibras* was completed, the hero of the story reappeared in *Butler's Ghost* as a man about town. He is no longer a fairy figure in some sort; he pretends to be a man like other men and to represent their vices in his own natural person, rather than as a gigantic puppet. The technique and the tone of the comedy of manners then became a possible attribute of burlesque verse, and what may be termed the more elegant parts of *Hudibras* had a better chance of affecting polite literature. The main objection of the official critics to the work of Butler was, not that it was not able, but that it was on the whole not sufficiently elevated or sufficiently polite. Prior, whether intentionally or not, met this objection by writing hudibrastic verse in a thoroughly polished and abstract manner, with scarcely any visual strength in it at all. To the tone of the comedy of manners he added the tone of the familiar essay and of the personal letter; for actors he chose principally himself and his friends and gave them parts to speak, but no action. He trims objective statement with personal whimsey. He decorates his verse with chaste antitheses and gives the burlesque parenthesis the air of a dramatic aside. He pens in his carefully studied informality of tone and phrase with precise fences of classical epigrammatic style. And all is done with the careful ease of the man of society. No mark of strain or labor must show. There must be no hint of ruggedness, of burliness in thought or form. In a sense, I suspect that Prior really ended the influence of *Hudibras* as a direct literary force; that he taught Swift and Gay a good deal of what they came to know about handling octosyllabics, and that hudibrastic verse as a polished instrument was generally recognized in the eighteenth century as the work of Prior rather than as the achievement of Butler.

Prior's bawdy tales form an exception in some particulars to the drift of the preceding statements, for in these, of course, he must have characters and actions. Both character and action are glossed with an easy expository manner and grave philosophy in the finest burlesque manner:

> Fabius, the Roman chief, who thus
> By fair retreat grew Maximus,
> Shows us, that all the warrior can do
> With force inferior, is Cunctando.[2]

I believe that Prior's volatility and verbal finesse are best displayed, however, in the first *Epistle to Fleetwood Shephard*, in *Alma*, and in that curious performance, *The Turtle and Sparrow*.

The *Epistle* shows the poet working in Butler's medium at a time when he had not succeeded fully in adapting the verse form to his own peculiar uses. In the nature of the case, he gives us epistolary playfulness, good humor, lightheartedness. But in a short poem he gives us also more direct echoes of Butler than he will later allow in a long one. Witness the accent of these couplets:

> For if his holiness would thump
> His reverend bum 'gainst horse's rump,
>
> Or, not to rove, and pump one's fancy
> For popish similes beyond sea;
> As folks from mud-walled tenement
> Bring landlords pepper-corn for rent;
> Present a turkey, or a hen,
> To those might better spare them ten.

[2] From *Paulo Purganti and His Wife*. All quotations from Prior's works are taken from the Aldine Edition, ed. by R. B. Johnson, London, 1892.

Or these:

> If once for principle 'tis laid,
> That thought is trouble to the head;
> I argue thus: the world agrees,
> That he writes well, who writes with ease:
> Then he, by sequel logical,
> Writes best, who never thinks at all.
>
> Egyptian gard'ners thus are said to
> Have set the leeks they after pray'd to;
> And Romish bakers praise the deity
> They chipp'd, while yet in its paniety.

Agility, self-assurance, variety, and a note of social grace are all present in this poem and will not be absent from the later productions. But by the time *Alma* was written Prior had had far more acquaintance with polite literature and conversation. Furthermore, he had the leisure that only a prisoner can know and could therefore let himself be led far into the diffuse fabric of an imaginary conversation.

Perhaps the chief difference between *Alma* and *Hudibras* is the difference in the temperaments of their authors. For one thing, Butler undoubtedly had a capacity for indignation which Prior lacked. For another, Butler's mind had a certain kind of philosophic sobriety and a weight of social and cosmic melancholy which are lacking in Prior's. Writing comes near to being Butler's life; to Prior it is a polite diversion. To Butler skepticism is necessary but regrettable; to Prior skepticism is the fabric of the day and an opportunity for wit. The problem of knowledge is a serious matter to Butler; to Prior it is a chance for some of the best fooling in English verse. The result of these opposite dispositions is that Prior gives to his hudibrastic verse almost everything but weight. He brought poetry into the drawing-room and found that certain essentials had to be left at the door if his remarks were to be appropriate to the place and the company. Prior addresses Alma:

How little gives thee joy or pain;
A print, a bronze, a flower, a root,
A shell, a butterfly can do't;
Ev'n a romance, a tune, a rhyme,

. . .

And cards are dealt, and chess-boards brought,
To ease the pain of coward thought:
Happy result of human wit!
That Alma may herself forget.

Hudibras addresses Sidrophel thus in the *Heroical Epistle:*

And all the best that can befal
An Artificial Natural,
Is that which Madmen find, as soon
As once th' are broke loose from the Moon
And proof against her Influence,
Relapse to ere so little Sense
To turn stark Fools, and Subjects fit
For sport of Boys, and Rabble-wit.

Clearly, Prior has the advantage in the decorum of his phrases; just as clearly Butler has an unprettified force and an unaffected sincerity which Prior cannot command. I believe that Prior described his own method justly in the third canto of *Alma* where his interlocutor is made to say:

Atoms you cut, and forms you measure,
To gratify your private pleasure;
Till airy seeds of casual wit
Do some fantastic birth beget:
And, pleas'd to find your system mended
Beyond what you at first intended,
The happy whimsey you pursue,
Till you at length believe it true.
Caught by your own delusive art,
You fancy first, and then assert.

By this method of fancy and assertion, Prior carried hudibrastic verse as far as it could be carried in the polite vein—so far, indeed, that in some passages we forget to call it burlesque writing. We find that instead we are reading what we have come to call society or light verse—a type that admits of no melancholy and no didacticism, while it plays neatly and airily with notions. The peroration of *Alma* is half sententious, half sad, but not enough of either to sour the good temper of the poem as a whole. That worldly good temper is, as I have suggested, one of the main points of difference between *Alma* and *Hudibras*.

In their subjects, on the other hand, the poems present a surprising and meaningful parallel. *Hudibras* may be taken as an anatomy of political tomfoolery; *Alma* as a survey of philosophic tomfoolery. Both are burlesques of the purely abstract and the purely literal approach to truth; both satirize false intellectual pretensions. *Hudibras* is richer and more complicated in its themes; for these Butler goes behind the face of contemporary politics to the varieties of mind that are responsible for so much political confusion. *Alma* is a slighter fabric, more delicately woven, with narrower borders. Not only Butler, but Horace, not only Horace, but Herrick, are blended in the verse. The poem satisfies the skepticism of a new age that has its doubts even of rationalism; it meets Prior's demand for the precise and delicate in statement, and it meets the Augustan requirement of refinement and clarity and completeness in design and in phrase.

The blend of qualities in *Alma* is notably lacking in the elegiac tale, *The Turtle and the Sparrow*, occasioned by the death of Prince George. It is hard to see why Prior wrote the poem at all, but since he did we have another chance to observe the variety of tone of which the octosyllabic line is capable. The turtle, of course, moans in true pastoral fashion; the garrulous sparrow tries to give comfort by relating his marital misadventures. He does so by talking in many balanced and closed couplets in as dull a succession of speeches as any heroic dramatist ever wrote, and is guilty of some passages which may be called either juvenile or imbecile in style according to the reader's taste. Of this mood the best example is

> I woo'd my cousin Philly Sparrow,
> O' th' elder house of Chirping End,
> From whence the younger branch descend.

When genealogical gossip and the bedtime story combine against him, the stoutest reader may be forgiven if he flees to pleasanter company.

This poem is worth mention only because it illustrates so well the versatility—and the undependability—of the medium in which it is written, and the difficulty of controlling it consistently. Hudibrastic verse could never be quite the same Pegasus again after Prior had finished currying and clipping it. He gave it a personal, conversational tone and made of it a suave vehicle for story or discussion. He brought *Hudibras* up-to-date, and in *Alma*, without any machinery but that of a mock-philosophic dialogue, made a poem as elegant and as representative as *The Rape of the Lock*. His achievement was indeed so thorough that in his adaptation of the medium he almost exhausted its possibilities for interesting abstract exposition and argument. I have no doubt that Gay learned some lessons in versifying from him and that those lessons helped to make the *Fables* so able and so dull. Nor is there much doubt that Swift found hints for his fluent epistolary poems not in the manner of Butler, but in that of Prior.

If hudibrastic verse tends to go to seed in the garden of Dean Swift—and I think that it does—part of the explanation can be found in the example of Prior and part in the subjects and the moods of Swift himself. Both Butler and Prior at their best chose subjects of weight for their burlesques. Swifts' masterly burlesques are in prose. For verse he reserves his personal chatter—about himself, his friends, his women. His eloquence becomes garrulity. He is a Cavalier in a Dean's frock, and is now embarrassed, now resentful, now wickedly pleased at his dual rôle. His verse a rather bewildering record of the prig, the sophomore, the misogynist, and the courtier; the dean seems never to have made his peace with women, or found it without them. The pastoral vein, sincere or burlesque, was of no special advantage to him, and the general satires, such as that *On Poetry*, with its occasional bits, are not distinguished. Swift is at his best when most personal—in his short descriptive pieces on his domestic life, and in the poem on his death. And in recounting the familiar in a familiar tone of voice he shows us another terminus of the burlesque mood. As abstract burlesque tends toward light verse and thereafter toward flimsy verse; descriptive burlesque tends toward realistic description. In both cases, the fantastic elements—the unfamiliar and the unreal—fall away, and leave behind them a technique which has its roots chiefly in careful observation and the reporting of the contemporaneous. We leave, for example, the fanciful burlesques and grotesques of Butler and Swift, and come to the realistic burlesques of Hogarth and Fielding.

In summing up those few burlesques which have been written with little or no fable behind them, we see that the type does not hold in it the promise of a long and well-developed life. The distinctive and interesting English burlesques are built on a story or fable. Where that element is lacking the burlesque diverges the more readily into the sententious, or the oratorical, or the personal. The pure burlesque of ideas is at its best in *Alma;* later on, if fancy was to be drawn fine, it would be by preference drawn into the familiar essay in prose.

IX

NARRATIVE BURLESQUE

Looking back from *Alma* to the works in imitation of *Hudibras* that had appeared sixty years before, we see at once that the strong burlesque tradition was the narrative tradition. We shall now follow that as far as it relates to Butler. It is at once clear that the poems discussed in Part Two belong in this class. In addition to those burlesques which attempted to cling very closely to the hudibrastic tradition on the whole, both in form and point of view, there are a large number of other poems, long and short, dull and clever, which represent more clearly the reciprocal relations between Butler's literary style and other literary fashions. For convenience we shall look first at the *Posthumous Works*, since that publication, while purporting to be the work of Butler, really gives an extraordinarily good idea of the uses to which his medium was put in transient poems written after his work had been finished.

This book also gives us a notion as to what Butler's work was supposed to be like in the mind of the collector of the pieces in the volume. Since the work, originally published in 1715, reached its sixth edition in 1754, it represented Butler's writing outside of *Hudibras* for a considerable time. The range of style is wide. Shirley's poem, "The glories of our birth and state," appears as *A Thought upon Death, after Hearing of the Murder of King Charles I*. That melancholy and sententious lyric is neighbored by a fine satirical song, *The Turncoat*, beginning

> I lov'd no king since forty-one,
> When prelacy went down,

> A cloak and band I then put on,
> And preach'd against the crown.

It is certainly to Butler's credit that he was assumed to be the author of these two poems, and not especially to his credit that the bulk of the hudibrastic poems in the volume were fathered on him.

Most of these burlesques are satires on Charles II and his court or refer frequently to their characteristics. *The Fable of the Lyon and the Fox. Alluding to the Cause and Manner of the Great Rebellion in the Year 1641* is obviously loyalist in temper, and relates the steps by which the king lost his inheritance. *Hudibras at Court* is a mixed performance, written, I should judge, in the late 1660's. It pretends in the earlier part to continue the burlesque of Hudibras and Ralpho on their return from the wars. They have had enough of fighting, but they reflect that it would be unprofitable to carry nothing but their bruises home with them. Furthermore, it is doubtful whether they should remain loyal to the rebellion. Hudibras says, that, since the saints have

> Attempted to assasinate
> And cut the throats of church and state,

he sees danger for them unless they change their clothes and their opinions. Thereupon they hide their arms in a hollow tree and go to gain favor with the restored king.

Thereafter the poem is devoted to reproving Charles. Hudibras the turncoat becomes a trusted member of his court and of the court of one of Charles's concubines. Ralpho declines any favor in a court "Where none but whores and villains rise." He despises a place in which the king's friends, the Cavaliers, have little chance and in which the king's traditional foes are flattered out of policy.

The writer of the poem indulges in a curious play on the word *Hudibras* in order to account for the success of the hero at court, and thus incidentally perpetuated the story of Butler's failure at the same place.

> This prince, whose ready wit and parts
> Conquer'd both men and women's hearts,
> Was so o'ercome by knights and Ralph,
> That he could never claw it off.
> He never eat, nor drank, nor slept,
> But *Hudibras* still near him kept,
> Never would go to church, or so,
> But *Hudibras* must with him go,
> Nor yet to visit concubine,
> Or at a city-feast to dine,
> But *Hudibras* must still be there,
> Or all the fat was in the fire.
> Now after all was it not hard,
> That he should meet with no reward.
> That fitted out this knight and squire,
> This monarch did so much admire:
> That he should never reimburse
> The man for th' equipage and horse,
> Is sure a strange ungrateful thing
> In any body but a king.

The same critical mood is maintained and strengthened in *Good Advice in Bad Times* and in *The Court Burlesqu'd*, two virulent satires on Charles. The first warns him against the people, the Commons, and Shaftesbury. With some irony, he is advised to "Be watchful of the factious city," and to control it by kissing its "ladies, like a king, And keep 'em poor by borrowing." For the most part, however, the poem is direct, hard-hitting, and intolerant.

> Some must be banish'd, others swing,
> Or thou must cease to be a king.
>
> . . .
>
> The Tories love thee and obey thee,
> None but the rebel Whigs betray thee,
> The stubborn wicked spawn of those
> That struggl'd for the good old cause.

Monmouth must be banished:

> The stallion of thy court Whitehall:
> Who got, great Charles, by thee, retains
> Thy princely lust, but wants thy brains.

The Court Burlesqued contains character sketches of some court figures—Clarendon, Buckingham, and Shaftesbury among them, but it is mainly given to an exposition of the personal habits of the king. The theme is conveniently expressed in three lines:

> O C—s! how happy had we been
> Hadst thou but had a fruitful queen,
> Or else been gelt before fifteen.

A group of other poems in hudibrastic verse are devoted more directly to the political crimes of Dissent: *The Character of a Fanatick*, *Dunstable Downs*, *The Whigs Ghost*, and *The Characters of the Five Sectaries*, viz. *Presbyterian, Independent, Anabaptist, Quaker, and Fifth Monarchy-Men*.

An Essay and *The Quarrel between Frank and Nan* are short stories or incidents in verse.

None of these poems was written by Butler; none has any sustained merit in idea or execution; none of the poems dealing with Dissent contains any fresh material. Yet the poems on the sects indicate the kind of subject popularly connected with Butler's tradition, and the *Posthumous Works* as a whole suggests the variety which Butler was supposed to be capable of producing. The hudibrastic poems show also the uses to which that verse was put. Direct satire, satirical sketches of actual people, satiric narrative, and a general atmosphere of realism are some of the chief characteristics of hudibrastic verse as soon as it leaves Butler's hands.

The strength of this realistic tendency is shown very early in the spurious *Second Part* of *Hudibras*. In this poem the knight and his squire are present in full character and panoply, and one might expect that a production designed to capitalize the success of Butler's *First Part* would have striven for similar atmosphere even more than for identical characters. But this effect the anonymous poet could not achieve. Instead, he packs his poem with action and with a succession of pictures of low life.

The opening incident is the description of a Maypole celebration and the charge of the reformers upon it. The May procession is headed by Bushero, Shanco, Butlero, Coquo, Sartoro, Trituratoro, Molindario, Lanio, Tergo, Pistoro and Thatchero. Then follows Cartero with the Maypole itself loaded on a dung cart:

> Poles so good, cut out by Art,
> And ornamented with no less
> Than Ribbons given by Doll, and Bess,
> And others of the Fairy–crew,
> Of Colours red, white, black, and blew,
> Yellow, cinnamon, and green,
> Here, and there, Nosegay between,
> Likewise many a Wedding Garter,
> Tickling Lasses into Laughter.

With this passage the poem springs to life. The first pages are consumed in a long confused passage on the general meaning of the May festival, and it is not until the author gets an actual scene before his eye that he can proceed with spirit and clarity. After the pole follow the girls —laundry girls, chambermaids, and dairymaids:

> Meg, and Kate, and Doll, and Joan,
> Buxome Lasses every one;
> With Peg, and Lett, and Luce, and Betty,
> For her face and foot call'd pretty;
> Moll, and Sall, and Nan, and Frank,
> Wenches free, and fat ith' flank:
> On Agnes Eve they'd strictly fast,
> And dream of those had kist 'em last;
> On St. Quintins watch all Night,
> With Smock hung up, for Lovers sight.

The whole company is on the way to the green at Kingston-on-Thames, famous for Hocktide games, and there Hudibras has just alighted from his horse for dinner at the inn. He sees the crowd approaching and after some thought decides not to attack it at once.

> No, quoth he, as I'm a Sinner:
> Let 'em wait till I do come,
> Charity begins at home:
> Serve self first, the Commonweal
> May stay till I have made my meal.

He thereupon sits down to eat with two companions. One is the commander of the forces of the Commonwealth stationed at Cheshire, "Guilielmo Knight Sir B—ton," who "had a face as Rocund as Horses." The other is a local justice who understands the law only because he is fortunate enough to employ a clerk "that might pass for an Intelligible Ass."

After dinner these three with their squires ride to the green to discuss how the attack on the celebration shall be made. They agree that reason should be their first weapon, and accordingly Hudibras addresses the crowd in part as follows:

> Have you to scoure a scurvy Cliffe
> Brought Gyants Tool from Teneriffe
> Ossa or Pelion? No, quoth Tergo,
> 'Tis for the Sisters, Ruth and Pergo,
> And such as follow Conventicle,
> No Brother has a Tool so mickle.

In the dispute Hudibras is threatened with a beating and when the justice reminds the crowd that he has legal power to have the pole pulled down, he is told plainly that the mob relies not on him but on its own strength; whereupon the knights and the justice are pulled from their horses, beaten and ridden back to town on "coltstaffes," their horses being driven in the rear.

When the companions are again in safety they consider methods of revenge. The rage of Hudibras can be quenched only after a goblet of sweetened French wine; he then proposes that a complaint be made to Parliament where, he says, he has a "special Friend." Sir William suggests that a message be sent to his troop at Nantwich. In either case, however, the rabble would be gone before the troops arrived, and the soldiers could do no more than cut down the pole. The justice is appealed to for local aid but he confesses himself "well contented with his blows" and will not act. He says also that they themselves have been guilty of disturbing the peace and that the case might go against them if brought to trial. Hudibras reviles him for cowardice, but when Sir William points out that their present position is none too safe he makes ready to depart, leaving his curse behind:

> Quoth Hudibras, to horse, a Curse
> Upon this Town, Malignants Nurse,
> And doth derive part of its name
> From whom (at first) Tyranny came.
> May darkness seize upon your dwellings,
> That have eclips'd my high Excellings;
> May all your Wives be leapt by Clown,
> And your fine Bread be turn'd to Brown;
> May all your cattel dye oth' Rot,
> And not a piece be had for Pot,
> Or Spit; and may your children mutter,
> When Kine want milk, and they want Butter.

For such a curse the Justice, who is left behind, calls him a Turk, a Jew, or a Philistine, but certainly no Christian.

Hudibras and Sir William ride with their squires to another town

> famous for Hogs,
> Butchers, and their like, Mastiff-dogs;
> And for a Witch that once liv'd there,
> Not unlike Falstaffe in Shakespeare;
> But more for fight, when Londoners
> In Thames were dipt or'e head and ears,
> And some Limbless in carts were sent,
> As Presents unto Parliament.

About a mile outside the town they find beside the road a stage about fifteen feet high, with a curtain.

> On either side of Theater
> Were plac'd two Tubs of sturdy Beer,
> And Wenches that for Novelties,
> Sold Ginger-bread, and Pudding-pies.

On the stage the showman is crying his cure for several ailments, accompanied by "Sir Capon and his Wench." Hudibras wishes to attack the ungodly assembly at once, but he is restrained by Sir William, who says that the showman by his gestures and rolling eyes is no doubt "A blest Tipe oth' Commonweal" and engaged in holy work. Accordingly the companions ride nearer and hear the discourse:

> Begar we kill you all, an den
> Presan make you alive agen;
> Wi dis me do all de gran Cure,
> De Pock, de Scab, de Calenture;
> Me make de Man strong, pour de Wench.
> (Then riseth Capon from the Bench)
> Look you me now, do you no see
> Dead yesterday, now live day be,
> Four boon, dey leap, dey dance, dey sing,
> Ma foy, an do de toder ting:
> Begar good Medicine do all dis.
> Capon makes legs, and wench doth kiss,
> Take hands, and throw their legs about.

Hudibras cries out and charges the medicine show with drawn pistol. The audience scatters, upsetting pies, spilling the beer and the custards and breaking the gingerbread knights and ladies that had been for sale. The squires fill their pockets with pies and Hudibras feels that he has regained his lost honor. The mountebank and his assistants are taken prisoner and are led into the town, where at the inn, Ostlero and Chamberlano are roused to attend the company.

The description of the interior is one of the realistic catalogues which form the chief interest of the poem. Rushes are scattered on the floor, boughs fill the fireplace and

> The Walls, in stead of Tapestry,
> Were hung about with History,
> As those of the Prodigal Son,
> And Judgment just of Solomon,
> In Capitals most fairly writ,
> To take the Eye, and help the Wit;
> Upon the Ceilings one might see
> Clouds of Mens names in Candlery,
> Who had been patrons of the place,
> And penny spent in putting Case;
> In Window laid was Lavendare,
> Of which the Cushions smelt most rare,
> With pots of Flowers very pleasing
> To put a Man into a sneezing.

The table in the center is covered with carpet spotted with ale and burnt with tobacco. Stools are placed about it with a chair of some dignity at one end. The candles are in tin sticks polished bright as silver. The description of the bed is as witty as it probably is faithful:

> At end of Room a bed did stand,
> Whose Posts were carv'd by cunning hand,
> Faces good store, but ne'r a Nose,
> And Legs too, without Feet or Toes,
> Which either came by some disaster,
> Or else he was not his Arts master;
> And yet perhaps he did express
> The Art he had in ugliness;
> For to do things exactly ill
> Must needs shew (though not judgment) skill:
> About the Teaster of the Bed,
> And so on that they call the Head,
> Were painted Bats (like Cherubs) flying,
> To comfort Souls when they are dying.
> But rouze my Muse, y'ave been too long
> Upon the Bed, pursue you Song.

After eating, Hudibras sets his chair below the painting of Solomon and prepares to judge his prisoners. He tries to frighten them by frowning and, when unsuccessful, whispers to Sir William, gesturing so emphatically that

Capon swears he belongs to their profession. Hudibras then roars and bites his thumb at the prisoners and wants to know who they are and whence. England, he says, is no place for vagrants. He suspects that they have come to stir up further trouble between the Cavaliers and the Commonwealth. Can they show any permits signed by Oliver or the Parliament? The mountebank defends himself by saying that having "got de hands of Kings" he does not need those of Oliver and Parliament, that he is a skilled physician and a French subject and should not be interfered with.

Hudibras learns that Capon has no trade. He then wants to know whether the wench is a man or a woman and orders the squires to strip her. When Capon protests that she is his wife, Hudibras cries out piously

> Squires forbear,
> And touch not the forbidden Ware.

He then grows sleepy and wishes to find some quick and moderate way of arriving at justice. He orders that no harm shall be done the prisoners and that they may go free if they will pay all the charges at the inn and if they will throw up their caps and cry "Long live our Noble Enemy." The Frenchman refuses but finally agrees to pay all the next morning, since it is against all custom to pay inn charges before the guests leave. Hudibras releases them on parole with the additional stipulation that the doctor bring him a plaster for his corn in the morning.

Hudibras is of course outwitted. The "prisoners" leave before Hudibras and his men are awake, having first taken care to pick the pockets of the squires and carry away all the hats and cloaks of the party.

Hudibras is awakened next morning by a trumpet blown under his window as a prelude to the fair which is opening in town that day. He and Sir William run out to find their prisoners and to destroy the fair. They see

> the deadly sins . . .
> Jane Shore's disgrace, and lamentation,
> (A Concubine not now in fashion)
> Then David, and Uriah's Wife,
> And Doctor Faustus to the Life.

They attack the show and the attendants flee, leaving behind their clothes and money, which are appropriated. The squires are especially furious on thinking of their recent losses so that

> Then the Puppets went to wrack;
> They cut what e're they hit upon,
> Down comes the Tower of Babylon.
> Quoth Fellow, Pox upon you, Sir,
> For spoiling Nebuchadnezer,
> His Nose was cut out ill before,
> But now you have abus'd it more,
> How think you after this disgrace
> Hee's able to look Beast in face?

The destruction is put an end to by the local butchers who are attending the fair. They set their dogs on the horses of Hudibras and Sir William, the squires run home, and the knights are thrown to the ground and knocked senseless. With this action the poem ends.

Its chief strength lies in the rapidity of its action and, as noted before, in its succession of pictures from contemporary life. Although some allowance may be made for exaggeration, the reader feels that there is no distortion of essentials in the Maypole scene, the presentation of the sideshow, the interior of the inn, or the fair. On the other hand, satire against the Commonwealth party is only incidental and while definite enough, it is not particularly severe.

While the action in Butler's poem is incidental to the meaning of it, here action is the meaning and the justification of the entire poem. And although we may sympathize with the author of *Hudibras* at seeing his title and his characters appropriated by a literary opportunist, we must admit that this able thief helped to set the style for a long succession of realistic poems on the times in hudibrastic dress.

The dramatic and pictorial elements in the work of D'Urfey have already been mentioned. This was followed by a number of poems before the long publications of Ned Ward appeared; while these have some political color about them, they are interesting principally because the writers of them have tried to expose contemporary manners. The poems of John Dennis, and of Richard Ames, are sufficiently representative of that kind of burlesque sketch in verse which apparently enjoyed a certain popularity in the 1690's.

The prose of Dennis is better reading than his verse. His *Poems in Burlesque* are a good example of the theory that curious or misshapen characters copied from life give as pleasant a burlesque effect as characters created by the imagination of the author; and in their execution the poems exemplify the weakness of that theory. In "The Triumviarte," three men brawl in a tavern with a woman

> Who, being Offensive to the Nose
> Is by Antiphrasis call'd Rose.

"In a Days Ramble in Covent-Garden," we are given glimpses of the "Counterfeit and State" virgins in church, of the beaus and wits at Will's, and of Dryden,

> Whom Pegasus takes so much Pride in,
> He suffers few beside to ride him.

In "The Two Friends," Freeman and Wild, who have lain with the same woman, who in turn gives birth to a girl and a boy, quarrel about which child belongs to each.

Ames does better, particularly in his *Lawyerus Bootatus & Spurratus*, largely because of greater audacity of phrase and more expansive animal spirits. This poem is a picture of the crowds of lawyers, justices, and "Tatter'd Clients" streaming out of London for vacation. The poet himself gets away for three weeks, at the end of which time

> I myself must take my leave
> Of Cowley, Waller, Oldham, Cleave-
> Land, and beloved Hudibrass,
> To study Actions on the Case.

All of these poems are well enough in their way, but are highly incidental and suffer like most of their class from lack of ideas. Concerning the presentation of burlesque characters, it appears almost as though London were too small for the uses of early journalism. The reporters seem infrequently to have got beyond the presentation of general types, almost in the manner of the outdated character-writing; as a consequence the attention of the modern reader is dulled. This tendency is most compactly shown in *A Rod for Tunbridge Beaus*, which in a succession of character sketches gives us the cosmetic beau, the pigmy beau, the fat beau, the dandy beau, and many others, in undramatic parade.

Of all the satiric reporters who used burlesque verse, Ned Ward is the best known, and, in a way, deservedly so. By no means as subtle a writer as Pitcairne, nor as felicitous as D'Urfey or three or four of those anonymous writers whose works are almost totally forgotten, he surpasses them all in physical self-assurance and tireless facility in the hudibrastic verse form. His verse has the same defects and excellences as his prose. The reader of *The London Spy*, for example, is amazed and delighted at the high-spirited flow and knowingness and clear observation in the opening pages. He thinks he is being introduced to an unusually eloquent writer. The writer is indeed unpracticed—he appears now to ape Sir Thomas Browne and now to improve upon Defoe—but he seems to have a wit of his own and ultimately will not be beholden to anyone. This first impression fades. We find that the author has no real variety of observation, that he lacks ideas, and that he is therefore redundant and, when taken in large doses, stupefying. But we still cannot deny the limited authority and vigor of isolated descriptive passages; and the same holds true of his verse.

Hudibras Redivivus contains many passages which show Ward's particular virtues and which best illustrate the entirely realistic use of burlesque verse. Here is a scene in a coffeehouse:

> Ent'ring, I saw quite a round Table,
> An ill-look'd thin-jaw'd, Calves-head, Rabble,
> All stigmatiz'd with Looks like Jews,
> Each arm'd with half a Sheet of News:
> Some sucking Smoak from Indian Fuel,
> And others sipping Turkey Gruel;
> Still searching after something new
> In Nob, the Gazette, or Review.
> Sometimes they smil'd, as if well pleas'd,
> Then by and by look'd vex'd and teaz'd,
> Alt'ring their sublunary Looks
> According as they lik'd their Books.

Again the author goes

> Stepping one Night into this House,
> When tipling Saints strong Ale carouse,
> And aged Sots, with shaking Hands,
> Liquor at once their Lips and Bands.

We can see how contemporaries may have got a pleasant sense of recognition from his verse and we can see also its repetitiousness in subject and lack of variety in diction.

Ward's later poem, *Vulgus Britannicus*, seems better because it is shorter, but it shows really no difference in style. In fact, the probability is that Ward all but exhausted the possibilities of the hudibrastic poem for journalistic purposes, just as, on the abstract side, Prior was to change the tradition by the very excellence of his performance. The truth is that in the field of realism, both actual and pretended, stronger forces were at work than any that could be derived from Butler. The realistic imitators, from the anonymous author of the *Second Part* up to Ward, were working under a false idea of what could be accomplished with the octosyllabic couplet. It was not adapted to the infinite detail and flexibility which the success of the realistic manner depends upon. These authors could not hope to compete with stage comedies; still less could they match the spaciousness of the novel and the book of adventure, or the complexity of the familiar essay. No better example of the limitations inseparable from this verse form can be found than Ward's "translation" of *Don Quixote* into octosyllabic verse. His version is of course much shorter than the original, yet it fills two fat little volumes. It is still too long, and too monotonous, in spite of the sprightly movement of many passages. The hudibrastic manner remained good for short flights of description and action, but proved nearly useless for sustained work undertaken on the theory that faithful presentation of actual life was sufficient for gaining a burlesque effect.

It is significant that Swift, the only great burlesque artist between Butler and Byron, did in Gulliver practically everything which the conscious imitators of Butler neglected. First of all, he eschewed verse; being committed to prose, he began to write prose at its most prosaic—that is he gave up all attempt at surprise in word and phrase, creating his world of the burlesque, the poetical, and the grotesque, behind the calm decision of his sentences. This is said not by way of reproving Ned Ward for not having been born Jonathan Swift; it is merely another way of saying again that first-rate burlesque treatment requires a mixture of the fantastic and the unearthly. Any lesser degree of tampering with the face of reality may produce something witty, amusing, even astonishing, but it will not provide the cosmic incongruity of the true burlesque.

What is the general character of burlesque writing during the eighteenth century? First, its strong literary flavor. *Hudibras* itself is in part a parody and, in the burlesque verse form outside the hudibrastic tradition, the travesty was dominant. Not only in classical travesty, but in the many ways in which the former literary manners were adapted, we follow a line of development that brings us to the point of triteness and boredom, and another line which brings us to the borders where translation, imitation, and burlesque are closely intermingled. It is not for nothing that Mr. Whibley's chapter in the *Cambridge History* is headed "Translators and Writers of Burlesque."

The tendency of poetical burlesque was to concern itself more and more with the superficial and the trivial—to deal with the surfaces of ideas rather than to grapple with the ideas themselves.

Other marks of the burlesque were an increased personal and casual flavor, a moralistic and realistic rather than an intellectual and a fantastic tone. Swift and Butler by quite different literary means arrive at a high fantastic illusion for purposes ultimately satiric. When that quality reappears after Swift it is used as in the Terror novels, to achieve synthetic nervous thrills, or in romantic lyrics to intensify the expression of a personal experience. But by the time of Byron it has pretty well dropped out of satiric practice.

The "burlesque" of Hogarth is, centrally, faithful drawing, line by line, of the subject of his moral satire—subjects of no very elevated social rank. In the corners of his pictures, in incidental decorations, he lets himself go and produces those approximations and distortions of the human face and form which are vital to true burlesque. But one needs only to read the text of *Hudibras* and then to look at Hogarth's illustrations of it to sense a great discrepancy. Hogarth drew the characters as though they were citizens—actual people—when to do so, as it seems to me, is to ignore the entire stylistic effect of Butler's original.

Fielding, again, has considerable to say about burlesque, and he had undoubtedly won the right to use the word by his long practice on the stage. But as it turns out in his actual work, his characters, both on the stage and in the novels, are little different from what we should call realistic types; indeed it is greatly to Fielding's advantage that they are as they are. He was in his place near the beginning of a new tradition, not at the end of an old one. For us the significant thing is that Fielding claims to be writing in *Joseph Andrews* neither a comic romance, nor a burlesque, although he says that the ridiculous is the object of burlesque and "The Ridiculous only . . . falls within my province in the present work." The apparent difficulty is explained by the author's remark that in *Joseph Andrews* he will limit burlesque to "our diction," having "carefully excluded it from our sentiments and characters: for there it is never properly introduced, unless in writings of the burlesque kind, which this is not intended to be." Fielding them, made his burlesque only a matter of words, deserting general burlesque for the quite different emotional field of comedy. The satiric novelist is apparently going to find full occupation with varieties of actual people and their actions without dealing with monsters.

If the fantastic could not withstand the realistic, we must also say that in the verse of Charles Churchill, the last considerable hudibrastic poet in England, it could not withstand the didactic. Add to Churchill's didacticism, garrulity, local hits, and devious writing, and you have reason enough for the opacity of *The Ghost*. It is a pity that the poem is no better, for it is written with enough vigor for ten. It has the form of hudibrastic verse, some of the tone of Pope's tradition, and of nearly every other current as well. Nevertheless it gives better examples of late hudibrastics than those afforded by the soft jog trot of Peter Pindar.

Night, in her weeds, with bats and owls
(Her usual equipage of fowls),
Came forth; and, changing colour, Day
(According to her vulgar way),
Like fealthy Felons hang'd, alack!
Turn'd from deep red to dismal black.

These few lines, or any others from the interminable
journeys of Dr. Syntax, show clearly enough why the
Butlerian vein ran out. It was not certainly because later
artists could not write good poetical satire; it was because
those who set out to imitate Butler had only a superficial
notion of what the verse of *Hudibras* was and what was
required in order to write it. Trumbull had a pretty good
idea of it, as did the author of *The Modern Hudibras*, but in
general it was assumed that anything octosyllabic would
pass for it, if it were also slipshod, informal, and colloquial,
with no store of observation and fancy in it or behind it.
Modern burlesque becomes increasingly personal, literary,
realistic, direct, and today the chief memorial to the
genius of Butler—a memorial that does not even belong
entirely to him—is the sharp playfulness of light verse.

BIBLIOGRAPHY

Works of Samuel Butler

I HAVE consulted the following editions of the work of Samuel Butler. All quotations are from the Cambridge University editions.

Hudibras, ed. by A. R. Waller. Cambridge University Press, 1904.
Characters and Passages from Note-Books, ed. by A. R. Waller. Cambridge University Press, 1908.
Satires and Miscellaneous Poetry and Prose, ed. by René Lamar. Cambridge University Press, 1928.
Hudibras, ed. by Zachary Grey. 2 vols., London, 1744.
Hudibras. Troy, N. Y. 1806. [First American edition.]
Genuine Remains, ed. by R. Thyer. 2 vols., London, 1759.
Posthumous Works. Sixth ed., London, 1754. [B]

Hudibrastic Verse

The following list, though it does not pretend to completeness, is representative of the hudibrastic verse published between 1662 and 1830. I have marked "[B]" those titles already given in Bond's *English Burlesque Poetry.*

Academia: or, the Humours of the University of Oxford. London, 1691. [By Alicia D'Anvers?]
Ames, Richard, Female Fire-Ships, The, A Satyr against Whoring. London, 1691.
———— Jacobite Conventicle. London, 1692.
———— Lawyerus Bootatus & Spurratus. London, 1691.
———— Search After Claret. London, 1691.
Amhurst, Nicholas, Poems on Several Occasions. . . . London, 1720.
Arbuckle, James, Momus Mistaken, A Fable. Occasioned by the Publication of the Works of the Revd. Dr. Swift. . . . [n.p.] 1735.
Art of Preserving, The. A Poem. Humbly Inscribed to the Confectioner in Chief of the B-T-SH C-V-L-Y. London, 1759.
Asgill, John, An Argument Proving, That . . . Man May Be Translated. . . . London, 1700.
Association &c., The, of the Delegates of the Colonies, at the Grand Congress, Held at Philadelphia, Sept. 1, 1774, Versified. . . . By Bob Jingle, Esq.; Poet Laureat to the Congress . . . [n.p.] 1774.

Bedlam, a Ball, and Dr. Price's Observations on the Nature of Civil Liberty. . . . London, 1776.

Blunder of all Blunders, The, . . . Or, Gulliver Devour'd by Butterflies: or, the Fops Observation on Lilliput. . . . Dublin, 1726.

Brackenridge, H. H., Gazette Publications. Carlisle, 1806.

Br-d-Street Patriots, or the Impartial Judge. London, 1717. [B]

Butchers Answer to the Taylor's Poem, The: or, Their Whole Profession Unmasked. [n.p., n.d.]

Churchill, Charles, Poems, ed. James Lauer, London, 1933.

Cleland, William, A Collection of Several Poems and Verses, Composed upon Various Occasions, By Mr. William Cleland, Lieutenant Collonel to My Lord Angus's Regiment. [n.p.] 1697.

Coalitional Rencontre Anticipated, The; A Poetical Dialogue. . . . London, 1785.

[Cock, Samuel, pseud.], Hudibrasso, a Burlesque Opera of Two Acts, As it is Acted with Great Applause, at the Theatre-Royal at Voluptuaria. [n.p.] [1741?]

Collection of Poems, for and against Dr. Sacheverell, A. London, 1720.

Collection of State Songs, Poems, &c. That Have Been Publish'd since the Rebellion, A. . . . London, 1716.

Collection of The Newest and Most Ingenious Poems, Songs, Catches, &c. against Popery, A. Relating to the Times. . . . London, 1689. [Second, Third, and Fourth Collections followed in the same year.]

Colvil, S., Mock Poem, or Whiggs Supplication. London, 1710.

Common-Hunt, The, or, the Pursuits of the Pope. [n.p., n.d.]

Continuation of Hudibras in Two Cantos, A. Written in the Time of the Unhappy Contest between Great Britain and America, in 1777 and 1778. London, 1778.

Death and Burial of John Asgill, Esq., The. . . . Dublin, 1702.

Defence for the Ladies, A: or, The Virtues of the Broad Brim'd Hat, In Answer to the Hoop'd Petticoats. London. [n.d.] B.M. note "circ. 1720."

Dennis, John, Miscellanies in Verse and Prose. London, 1693.

——— Poems in Burlesque; with a Dedication in Burlesque, to Fleetwood Shepherd, Esquire. London, 1692.

Dialogue between the Ghost of A-l B-, and the Substance of a G-l, A; Shewing the Difference between a Chop and a Pop. London, [n.d.]

Dialogue Between the Miller and his Dogg, A. [n.p., n.d.]

Dialogue Which Lately Pass'd between The Knight and His Man John, A. London, [n.d.]

Dildoides, a Burlesque Poem. With a Key Explaining Several Names and Characters in Hudibras. Never Before Printed. London, 1706. [B]

Diluvium Lachrymarum. London, 1694.

Disappointed Marriage, The, or an Hue and Cry after an Outlandish Monster, The. [n.p., n.d.] [Vs. William of Orange.]

BIBLIOGRAPHY 173

Dissertation in Burlesque, The. London, 1701. [B]

Dixon, Richard, Canidia, or The Witches. A Rhapsody. In Five Parts. By R. D. London, 1683.

Dulcinead Variorum, The: a Satyrical Poem, in Hudibrastick Verse. . . . London, 1729. [B]

D'Urfey, Thomas, Butler's Ghost, or Hudibras the Fourth Part. London, 1682.

—— Collin's Walk through London and Westminster. London, 1690.

E–H's Instructions to Their Member. [n.p., n.d.]

Epipapresbyter. . . . London, 1685.

Epistle From Cambridge, An. *London Mag.*, IV (June, 1735), 332. [B]

Farewell, James, The Irish Hudibras, or Fingallian Prince. . . . London, 1689.

Fessenden, Thomas Green, Democracy Unveiled. Boston and New York, 1805.

—— Original Poems. London, 1803.

—— Pills, Poetical, Political, and Philosophical. Philadelphia, 1809.

—— Terrible Tractoration, The. London, 1803.

Fielding, Henry, Poems, etc. In *Works*. Vol. XI, ed. J. P. Browne. London, 1903.

Fight and No Fight, A, or The Mock-Duel in St. James's Park. London, [n.d.].

Four Hudibrastic Cantos. London, 1714. [B]

Four Satires. Viz. . . . On National Vices . . . On Writers . . . On Quakers . . . On Religious Disputes. . . . London, 1737.

Free-Thinkers. . . . London, 1711. [By Anne Finch?] [B]

Funeral Tears upon the Death of Captain William Bedloe. [n.p., n.d.]

Grand Enquiry, The; or, What's to be Done with Him? [n.p., n.d.]

Green, Matthew, The Spleen. An Epistle Inscribed to His Particular Friend Mr. C. J. . . . London and Dublin, 1737.

Heraldiad, The; A Satyr upon a Certain Philosopher. Containing a Description of the Grub-street Debate Held the 22nd of This Present Month. By Martin Gulliver. [n.p.] 1730.

Heroi-Comical Epistle from a Certain Doctor to a Certain Gentle-Woman, In Defence of the Most Antient Art of Punning, An. . . . London, [n.d.]

Hickeringill, Edmund, A Burlesque Poem In Praise of Ignorance. . . . London, 1708. [B]

History of an Election, The. Date Unknown. By Joshua Jinglejoints. [n.p., n.d.]

History of Colonel Nathaniel Bacon's Rebellion in Virginia, The. Annapolis, 1731. [B]

Hogan-Moganides: or, the Dutch Hudibras. London, 1674.

Hudibras, a Drama, Founded on the Poem of Butler. 1819. [Ms in Harvard Library. Merely an arrangement of quotations from Hudibras, with songs interpolated, parodying Romantic poets.]

[Hudibras, Hugh, pseud.], The Levellers; or, Satan's Privy-Council. [London?], 1793.

Hudibras. The Second Part. London, 1663. [Spurious.] [A second edition of the Spurious Second Part was published in the same year, with same pagination. Some changes in spelling are apparently the only differentiation. This was followed in the same year by a third edition, "Published to Undeceive the Nation." The third edition contains 123 pages instead of 100 as in the first two.]

Hudibras Answered by True de Case in his Own Poem and Language. [n.p., n.d.]

Hudibras in Ireland; a Burlesque on the Late Holy Wars in the Sister Kingdom. London [n.d.]

Hudibras On Calamy's Imprisonment and Wild's Poetry. To the Bishops. [n.p., n.d.]

[Hudibras the Younger, pseud.], Sultan Sham, and His Seven Wives. London, 1820.

――― Anti-Cant. An Extra Satirical Burlesque. Birmingham, 1824. [Reviewed in the *Birmingham Spectator*, Oct. 2, 9, 1824. Second ed., Birmingham, 1824. Attributed to Thomas Martin.]

Hue and Cry after Them Brewers, Who Raise Their Rates on Drink. Dublin, 1725.

Hyp, The, a Burlesque Poem in Five Canto's. . . . London, 1731. [B]

Illustrations of Hudibras: Sixty Portraits of Celebrated Political and Literary Characters, Imposters, and Enthusiasts, Alluded to by Butler in His Hudibras. London, 1821.

Inamorato and Misogamos: or, A Love-Song Mock'd. [n.p., n.d.]

In Imitation of Hudibras. The Dissenting Hypocrite, Or Occasional Conformist. London, 1704. [B]

Islington-Wells; or the Threepenny-Academy. London, 1691.

Jack and the Queen Killers. . . . London, 1820.

Jacobite's Hudibras. . . . London, 1692. [In prose.] [B]

Knave of Trumps Fell into the Dumps, The; Caleb Turn'd Physician, or a New Receipt for the Gripes. Printed for the Author of the Craftsman. London [n.d.]

Letter from an Apothecary's 'Prentice in W-Street to His Friend at Oxford, A. *London Mag.*, VI (Aug., 1737), 449–50. [B]

Liber Regalis, or the C-n. London, 1821.

Litchfield Squabble, The. . . . London, 1747. [B]

Lloyd, Evan, The Methodist. . . . London, 1766.

Love in the Suds; A Town Eclogue. . . . London, 1752.

Meston, William, The Knight. Edinburgh, 1723. [B]

――― The Poetical Works of William Meston. Edinburgh, 1767.

Methodists, The; An Humorous Burlesque Poem; Address'd to the Rev. Mr. Whitefield and His Followers. . . . London, 1739. [B]

Mitre, The; A Tale in Hudibrastick Verse. . . . London, 1731. [B]

Modern Hudibras, The; In Two Cantos. London, 1831.

Moffett, William, The Irish Hudibras, Hesperi-neso-graphia: or, a Description of the Western Isle. By W. M. Dublin, 1724. [B]

Norfolk Gamester, The. . . . London, 1734.

One-Eyed Coronation, The; or, a Peep into Westminster Abbey. London [n.d.].

On the Answer to Dr. Wilds Poem; upon Mr. Calamy's Imprisonment. [n.p., n.d.]

On the Dissolution of the Club of Voters. [n.p.] 1678.

Oxford Act, The. London, 1693.

P., T., Hickledy-Pickledy: or, The Yorkshire Curates Complaint. [n.d.]

P – and S –Fe–s of T–y C–e, Dublin, their A –s to the L –C –&c. [n.p., n.d.]

Panegyrick upon Oates, A. [n.p., n.d.]

Paragraph, Peter [pseud.], The Methodist, and Mimick; a Tale in Hudibrastick Verse. London, 1766.

Parallel betwixt Popery and Phanaticism, in a Letter to T. S. [n.p., n.d.]

Paraphrastical, Hudribrastical, Versification, A. . . . Gent. Mag., IX (Dec., 1739), 650. [B]

Parodies on Gay. To Which Is Added the Battle of the Busts, a Fable Attempted in the Style of Hudibras. London [1810?].

Patriots of North America, The. A Sketch. With Explanatory Notes. . . . New York, 1775.

Pendragon, or the Carpet Knight, His Calendar. London, 1698.

Pettifoggers, The. A Satire. In Hudibrastick Verse. . . . London, 1723. [B]

Phino-Godol. A Poem. In Hudibrastick Verse. . . . London, 1732. [B]

Pig and the Mastiff, The. Two Tales. London, 1724. [By Samuel Wesley the younger?]

Pindar, Paul, [pseud.], Fleaiad, The, an Heroic Poem, with Notes, Humbly Addressed to Peter Pindar. . . . London, 1787.

———— Jew-De-Brass. . . . London [n.d.]

Pitcairne, Archibald, Babell; a Satirical Poem on The Proceedings of the General Assembly in the Year M.DC.XCII. Edinburgh, The Maitland Club, 1830.

Plain Truth, or Downright Dunstable. London, 1740.

Poem, In Vindication of the Late Publick Proceedings, A; By Way of Dialogue, between a High Tory and a Trimmer. . . . 1689. [n.p.]

Poem Address'd to the Quidnuncs at St. James's Coffee House London, A; Occasion'd by the Death of the Duke of Orleans. [n.p.] 1724.

Poem on the Erecting a Groom-Porter's-House Adjoining to the Chapple, in the Castle of Dublin, A. [n.p., n.d.]

Priest in Rhyme, The; A Doggrell Versification of Kidgell's Narrative, Relative to the Essay on Woman. . . . London [n.d.]

Prior, Matthew, Poetical Works, ed. by R. B. Johnson. London, 1892. [B]

Priviledge of Our Saints In the Business of Perjury, The; Useful for Grand-Juries. By the Author of Hudibras. London, 1681.

Progress of Methodism in Bristol, The; or, the Methodists Unmasked. . . . London, 1743.

Prometheus, A Poem. Dublin, 1724.

Rape of the Bride, The; or Marriage and Hanging Go by Destiny; a Poem Hudibrastick. London, 1723. [B]

Remarks upon Remarks, on a Certain Lady and Her Sparks. [n.p., n.d.]

Renowned Quack Doctor's Advice to His Poetaster in Ordinary, The. *London Mag.*, VIII (Nov. 1739), 617–18. [B]

Rice, Woodford, The Rutland Volunteer Influenzad: or, a Receipt to Make a Portrait, a Soldier, or a Poet. London, 1783.

Risum Teneatis? Amici: or, A True and Diverting Account of a Late Battle Between a Priest and a Porter. In Hudibrastick Verse. . . . London, 1732.

Robin-Red-Breast's Answer to the Black-Bird's Song. . . . London, 1715.

Robin's Panegyrick. Or, the Norfolk Miscellany. London, [n.d.] [B]

Rod for Tunbridge Beaus, A. . . . London, 1701. [B]

R[oya]L Rumping!! or, The Courtly Insult to an Illustrious Personage. London, 1821.

Saint Paul's Church; or, the Protestant Ambulators. London, 1716. [B]

Saints Congratulatory Address, The. . . . London, 1718. [B]

Sarah-ad; or, a Flight for Fame, The. . . . London, 1742.

Satyrical Poem, A; or, the Beggar's-Opera Disected. London [advertised in *Fog's Weekly Journal*, April 5, 1729, p. 3, col. 1].

Satyrick Poem against the Mercenary Wretches . . . The Authors of Heraclitus and Observator, A. . . . London, 1682.

Satyr Satiris'd, an Answer to a Satyr on the Reverend D – n S – T. [n.p., n.d.]

Saylors Address to His Majesty, The. London, 1727.

Servitour, The; a Poem. Written by a Servitour of the University of Oxford. . . . London, 1709. [B]

Ship's Mate and the Parson, The; a Poem to His Grace the Lord Arch-Bishop of Dublin. [n.p., n.d.]

Sir Robert Brass: or, the Knight of the Blazing Star. A Poem. After the Manner of Hudibrass. . . . London, 1731. [B]

Sot-Weed Factor, The; or, A Voyage to Maryland. . . . London, 1708. [In *Early Maryland Poetry*, ed. by B. C. Steiner. "Maryland Hist. Soc. Pub.," No. 36.] [B]

Sotweed Redivivus; or, The Planter's Looking-Glass in Burlesque Verse Calculated for the Meridian of Maryland. Annapolis, 1730. [In *Early Maryland Poetry*, ed. by B. C. Steiner. "Maryland Hist. Soc. Pub.," No. 36.]

Strolling Hero, The; or, Rome's Knight Errant. . . . London, 1744. [B]

Stumbling Horse, The. Ascrib'd by a Friend to the Right H – e ———. [n.p., n.d.]

Swift, Jonathan, The Poetical Works. 3 vols., London, 1866.
Tauronomachia. . . . London, 1719. [B]
Thalia: or the Spritely Muse. . . . London, 1725. [B]
They Are All Mad, and Bewitch'd or, the Devil to Do at Westminster, and at St. James's. [n.d., n.p. circ. 1715.]
Tit for Tat . . . To Which Is Annexed an Epistle from a Nobleman to a Doctor of Divinity . . . Also The Review; or, the Case Fairly Stated on Both Sides. London, 1734.
To Caleb D'Anvers, Esq.; Or the Treaty Lately Concluded at Seville. [n.p., n.d.]
Tom Punsibi's Letter to Dean Swift. [n.p.] 1727.
Total Eclipse, The; a Grand Politico-Astronomical Phenomenon, Which Occurred in the Year 1820. London [1820?].
(Totne)ss (Ver)sified, (T)he. . . . Dublin, 1727.
Trip to Germany, A; or, the D. of M.–h's Farewell to England. [n.p., n.d.]
Trip to Leverpoole, A; By Two of Fate's Children. . . . London, 1706.
True Cause of a Certain G–1 Officer's Conduct, On the First of August Last, The; in Which All Former Explanations Are Explained Away. London, 1756.
Trumbull, John, Poetical Works. Hartford, Conn., 1820.
Tunstall, William, A Collection of Ballads, And Some Other Occasional Poems. . . . London, 1727.
Unequal Match, The; A Tale. By the Author of the Curious Maid. London, 1737.
Ungrateful World, The; or, The Hard Case of a Great G–1. [n.p., n.d.]
Villegas, Francisco de Quevedo, The Visions of Don Francisco de Quevedo . . . Burlesqued by a Person of Quality. London, 1702.
Ward, Edward, Delights of the Bottle, The; or, the Compleat Vintner. . . . London, 1720.
——— Hudibras Redivivus; or a Burlesque Poem on the Times. London, 1705–07.
——— Hudibrastick Brewer, The; or, a Preposterous Union between Malt and Meter. A Satyr upon the Supposed Author of the Republican Procession 1714. London, 1714. [Internal evidence indicates that Ward was the author of this poem.] [B]
——— Life and Notable Adventures of Don Quixote de la Mancha, The; merrily Translated into Hudibrastic Verse. Edinburgh, 2 vols., 1711–12.
——— London-Spy Compleat, The, in Eighteen Parts, by Ned Ward. The Casanova Society. London, 1924.
——— Miscellaneous Writings in Verse and Prose. 6 vols. London, 1717–24.
——— Northern Cuckold, The, or the Garden House Intrigue . . . with an Addition to the Delights of the Bottle; Or, the Compleat Vintner. . . . London, 1721.

Ward, Edward, Parish Gutt'lers, The: or, The Humours of a Select Vestry. London, 1722. [B]

——— Republican Procession, The; or the Tumultuous Cavalcade. London, 1714. [B]

——— Vulgus Britannicus; or the British Hudibras. London, 1710. [B]

Ward, Thomas, England's Reformation. . . . Hamburg, 1710. [B]

War with Priestcraft: or, the Free-Thinker's Iliad. A Burlesque Poem. . . . London, 1732. [B]

Way to Heaven in a String, The; or, Mr. A - 's Argument Burlesqued. . . . London, 1700. [B]

Whiggery Display'd; or, The Principles, Practices, Erudition and Religion of Our Modern Whiggs. . . . By a True Son of the Church of England. [n.p.]. 1719.

Whigs Address to His Majesty, The. [n.p., n.d.]

Whole Tryal, Examination, and Conviction of the Turnip-Man, The; before the Judges of the King's Bench Bar at Westminster Hall, on Monday the 30th of November, 1719. London [n.d.]

Your Servant Sir, or Ralpho to Hudibras Descanting on Wild's Poetry. [n.p., n.d.]

Historical and Critical Works

In addition to standard histories of literature and politics, I have consulted the following special books.

Baldwin, Edward Chauncey, "A Suggestion for a New Edition of Butler's Hudibras." *P.M.L.A.*, XXVI, 528–48.

Blunden, Edmund, "Some Remarks on Hudibras." *London Mercury*, XVIII, (June, 1928), 172–77.

Bond, Richmond P., English Burlesque Poetry, 1700–1750. "Harvard Studies in English," Vol. VI. Harvard University Press, 1932.

Bredvold, Louis I., The Intellectual Milieu of John Dryden. "Univ. of Michigan Publications, Language and Literature." Vol. XII, 1934.

Brunetière, Ferdinand, "La Maladie du burlesque." *Études critiques sur l'histoire de la littérature française*, Vol. VIII., Paris, 1907.

Butterfield, H., The Whig Interpretation of History. London, 1931.

Cook, Elizabeth Christine, Literary Influences in Colonial Newspapers, 1704–1750. New York, 1912.

Curtiss, J. T., Butler's Sidrophel. *P.M.L.A.*, XLIV, (Dec., 1929), 1066–78.

Day, Cyrus Lawrence, The Life and Non-Dramatic Works of Thomas Durfey. Harvard dissertation, 1930 (typed MS).

De Beer, E. S., The Later Life of Samuel Butler. *The Review of English Studies*, Vol. IV, No. 14, April, 1928.

Ellis, Harold Milton, Joseph Dennie and His Circle. Austin, Texas, 1915.

Fieling, Keith, British Foreign Policy, 1660–1672. London, 1930.

Fieling, Keith, History of the Tory Party, A. 1640–1714. Oxford, 1924.

Green, Richard, Anti-Methodist Publications Issued during the Eighteenth Century. London, 1902.

Grey, Zachary, Critical, Historical, and Explanatory Notes upon Hudibras, By Way of Supplement to the Two Editions Published in the Years 1744 and 1745. By Zachary Grey, LL.D. To Which is Prefixed, A Dissertation upon Burlesque Poetry. By the Late Learned, and Ingenious Montagu Bacon, Esq. And an Appendix Added; In Which is a Translation of Part of the First Canto of the First Book into Latin Doggrel. London, 1752.

Grub, George, An Ecclesiastical History of Scotland. Edinburgh, 1861.

Harris, Robert Brice, The Beast in English Satire from Spenser to John Gay. Harvard dissertation, 1930.

"Imitations of Hudibras." Retrospective Rev., III (1821), 317–35.

Jones, I. Deane, The English Revolution, 1603–1714. London, 1931.

Jones, Virgil Laurens, English Satire in the Latter Half of the Seventeenth Century. Harvard dissertation, 1911 (typed MS.)

Kinloch, M. G. J., Studies in Scottish Ecclesiastical History in the Seventeenth and Eighteenth Centuries. London, 1898.

Kirkton, James, The Secret and True History of the Church of Scotland, from the Restoration to the Year 1678. Edinburgh, 1817.

Kitchin, George, A Survey of Burlesque and Parody in English. Edinburgh, 1931.

Lee, Umphrey, The Historical Backgrounds of Early Methodist Enthusiasm. Columbia University Press, 1931.

Mathieson, William Law, Politics and Religion, a Study in Scottish History from the Reformation to the Revolution. Glasgow, 1902.

Newlin, Claude M., The Life and Writings of Hugh Henry Brackenridge. Princeton University Press, 1932.

Paul, H. G., John Dennis, His Life and Criticism. Columbia University Press, 1911.

Perrin, Porter Gale, The Life and Works of Thomas Green Fessenden, 1771–1837. "Univ. of Maine Studies," Second Series, No. 4, The Maine Bulletin, Vol. XXVIII, No. 7, Jan. 1926.

Previté-Orton, C. W., Political Satire in English Poetry. Cambridge University Press, 1910.

Quintana, Ricardo, "John Hall of Durham and Samuel Butler. A Note." Modern Language Notes, XLIV (March, 1929), 175–79.

——— Mind and Art of Jonathan Swift, Oxford University Press, 1936.

Sanderson, Robert, Episcopacy (As established by The Law in England) Not Prejudicial to Regal Power. . . . London, 1661.

Shaftesbury, Characteristics, ed. by J. M. Robertson, London, 1900.

Tucker, Robert Leonard, The Separation of the Methodists from the Church of England. Columbia University Press, 1918.

Veldkamp, Jan, Samuel Butler, the Author of Hudibras. Amsterdam, 1923.

Warner, Wellman J., The Wesleyan Movement in the Industrial Revolution. London, 1930.

Webster, C. M., Hudibras and Swift. *Modern Language Notes*, XLVII (April, 1932), 245–46.

West, Albert H., L'Influence française dans la poèsie burlesque en Angleterre entre 1660 et 1700. Paris, 1931.

Wodrow, Robert, Analecta. Edinburgh, 1842.

Wright, Thomas, Caricature History of the Georges. London, 1868.

—— History of Caricature and Grotesque in Literature and Art, A. . . . London, 1865.

INDEX